I Knit San Francisco

New York • Washington

A note about needles and gauge

We specified needle sizes and circular needle lengths used by the designers in each pattern to knit the items you see photographed on the following pages; they are not necessarily the sizes and lengths *you* will need to make yours. Use the needle size that allows you to achieve gauge.

It may not be your favorite thing, but we highly recommend a gauge swatch for all projects to avoid disappointment. For the garments, why not start a sleeve? If you achieve gauge, you already have part of a sleeve finished, and if you don't, it's not a huge amount of knitting. Don't forget to block your swatch before measuring your gauge.

If you prefer knitting small circumferences with the Magic Loop method, you will be most comfortable with needles that are 40 inches/100 cm or longer in the size that allows you to achieve gauge—Magic Loop can be done with 24-inch/60 cm needles, but longer is more comfortable. DPNs, two circulars, or short circulars are all viable options, so choose what works for you. For garments, especially those worked in the round, choosing a needle length *slightly* shorter than your desired circumference will make for a comfortable knitting experience for the body of the garment.

A note about yarn

We love the yarn choices our designers made for each pattern but know that it may be more difficult to find said yarns wherever you are in the world. To help you make yarn substitutions, we include yarn weight, yardage, and fiber content in each pattern.

On each pattern you will also find contact information for the company whose yarn was used, in case you would like to get your yarn from the original source. We are big fans of these yarnies and would love for you to support them.

I Knit San Francisco
Editors: Kathleen Dames & Alice O'Reilly
Pattern Photographer: Alli Novak | Luzography
Art Director & Graphic Designer: Kathleen Dames
Technical Editor: Laura Cameron
Illustrator: Laurel Johnson
Models: Bhavana Srinivas & Gowtham Ramachandran
Photography Assistants: Ryan James & Gowtham Ramachandran
Bay Area Photographers: Kathleen Dames & Alice O'Reilly; iStock.com/DianeBentleyRaymond, emyu, SerrNovik, bluejayphoto, encrier, M. Kaercher
Designers: Vilasinee Bunnag, Kathleen Dames, Faina Goberstein, Juliana Lustenader, Audry Nicklin, Sonya Philip, Yvonne Poon, Sloane Rosenthal, Heatherly Walker, Julie Weisenberger, Kelly White
Yarn Support: Bay Street Yarns, The Dye Project, Hudson + West Co., Little Skein in the Big Wool with help from Seismic Yarns, Love Fest Fibers, Sincere Sheep, Speckled Finch Studios, Twirl Yarn, A Verb for Keeping Warm

Copyright © 2019 One More Row Press
Photographs copyright © 2019 Alli Novak
Illustrations copyright © 2019 Laurel Johnson
All rights reserved. Patterns are for personal use only and not for resale or sharing. No part of this publication may be reproduced or transmitted in any form or by any means, electronic, mechanical, photocopying, recording, or otherwise, without prior written permission from the publisher.

Printed in the United States, United Kingdom, and Australia by IngramSpark.

ISBN: 978-0-578-58019-7

Direct all inquiries to *hello@onemorerowpress.com*.

Follow One More Row Press
Facebook: *fb.me/onemorerowpress*
Instagram: *@onemorerowpress*
Pinterest: *onemorerowpress*
Sign up for our newsletter on our website: *onemorerowpress.com*

To download, redeem at *ravelry.com/redeem/one-more-row-press*

IKSFOMR40GL35

10 9 8 7 6 5 4 3 2 1

Contents

5 Land Acknowledgment
6 Introduction

<u>Patterns</u>

9 *Continuous* by Kelly White
11 Kelly loves San Francisco
12 *Ruth Asawa* by Kelly White
15 *Ferry Building* by Sloane Rosenthal
19 Sloane loves San Francisco
21 *Fog City* by Faina Goberstein
23 Faina loves San Francisco
25 *Grant Avenue Stroll* by Yvonne Poon
28 Yvonne loves San Francisco
29 Kathleen loves San Francisco & Alice loves San Francisco
31 *Half-Moon* by Julie Weisenberger
33 Julie loves San Francisco
35 *Lombard Street* by Audry Nicklin
37 Audry loves San Francisco
39 *Mission Dolores* by Heatherly Walker
41 Heatherly loves Paradise (& SF)
43 *Painted Lady* by Sonya Philip
45 Sonya loves San Francisco
47 *Yerba Buena* by Juliana Lustenader
49 Juliana loves San Francisco
51 *18th & Castro* by Kathleen Dames & Vilasinee Bunnag
53 Vilasinee loves San Francisco

54 <u>The 3-Day Yarn Crawl</u>
56 *San Francisco*
   Atelier Yarns, Firebird Yarns, ImagiKnit, Britex
58 *Sonoma & Napa Counties and East Bay*
   Cast Away Yarn Shop, Yarns On First, Avenue Yarns, The Black Squirrel, A Verb for Keeping Warm
60 *Peninsula, Monterey Bay & Santa Cruz*
   The Royal Bee Yarn Company, Monarch Knitting, Yarn Shop Santa Cruz

62 Abbreviations, Stitches & Techniques
63 Contributors
64 Thanks!
65 Pattern Index

Land Acknowledgment

One of the definitions of the verb "to knit" is "to unite or cause to unite," as in, "disparate regions had begun to knit together." This act of knitting together means we consider our relationships with each other, and the land and waters of this region. We endeavor to honor the land and its peoples by acknowledging that this book was created and photographed on the traditional lands of the Ramaytush Ohlone people in what is now known as San Francisco.

Throughout the Bay Area, the Ohlone* are known for their intimate knowledge and use of natural fibers to construct housing and clothing, and they continue to create some of the most prized baskets in the world. As many of us seek to use more natural fibers in our work, we rely on amazing natural resources, and we look to the past and to those who still use traditional methods to raise sheep, shear sheep, and spin fiber into yarn to make something of use for future generations. We look to the Ohlone who continue to practice a reciprocal relationship with the land that we are on in order to honor the life lived and the gifts that are given.

Our ancestors were once indigenous to the land they came from, and we can honor and celebrate our various heritages while still acknowledging the Indigenous people of the land we are on. Through knitting, many have learned about their own culture, their heritage, and their own indigeneity. Through knitting, many have found community. Through knitting, many have learned and practiced sustainability and have developed a respect for the land and the life it supports.

The presence of settlers (non-Indigenous peoples who live on these lands) is not neutral; it has had and continues to have devastating impacts on many aspects of life for Indigenous peoples. We hold this understanding in our interactions and engagements with this land and its people. Settlers need to recognize that our knowledge and way of doing things may not be the priority as we work towards knitting together.

We would also like to acknowledge the Indigenous people on whose land the publishers are located. The Piscataway Conoy Tribe in what is now known as Silver Spring, Maryland, and The Lenape in what is now known as Manhattan.

—**Co-written by Scott Territo and Kanyon Sayers-Roods,**
Co-founders of Kanyon Konsulting LLC

Visit *https://kanyonkonsulting.com/ohlone-california-native-resources-introduction/* for a deeper dive into any of these topics.

---

*The term Ohlone is used to encompass a number of Indigenous peoples, including Ramaytush, Chochenyo, Tamien, Awaswas, Mutsun, Rumsen, Chalon, and Esselen. The Bay Area is also home to the Miwok to the North and Yokuts to the East.

Have you, too, left your heart in San Francisco?

We have! Having spent lots of time in the Bay Area over the years, we have an abiding affection for the place and people, and have come to the same conclusion: bring your woollies, even if you're visiting in August.

Mark Twain didn't say "the coldest winter I ever spent was a summer in San Francisco" (no one knows definitively who did), but frankly it could have been *anyone* who spent any time in the Bay Area microclimate on a summer day. Never downright freezing, the cool damp of the Pacific always moderates the weather, and a bit of woolly goodness, whether in accessory or garment, is always a welcome layer (despite what any polar fleece wearer might tell you).

San Francisco has changed over the years. Waves of migration have left their mark on this land and on this city. A place which was once the far end of the Gold Rush is now the starting place of tomorrow's innovations. Not all of the history is pretty, yet there is immense beauty (and pride) in this city.

We found inspiration in the geography, history, and meteorology of San Francisco: create your own version of Kelly White's **Continuous** shrug inspired by the fascinating art of Ruth Asawa (her wire sculptures have particular appeal to fiber artists—don't miss Kelly's introduction to Asawa on p. 12), meander down the switchback curves of **Lombard Street** in a sock with Audry Nicklin, then take a **Grant Avenue Stroll** through Yvonne Poon's personal history of Chinatown for a curved wrap thanks to German short rows, and keep your head warm with Faina Goberstein's slip-stitch **Fog City** hat, plus half a dozen more designs.

What better way to knit San Francisco than with local yarn? From **Sincere Sheep** up in Napa all the way down to **The Dye Project** in Santa Cruz, with **Little Skein in the Big Wool**, **A Verb for Keeping Warm**, **Love Fest Fibers**, and other talented dyers in between.

Where to find those yarns is our other favorite part of creating these books, and our geographic boundaries of "San Francisco" are generous, but as you can see there were people and places we couldn't leave out. From San Francisco proper to the Berkeley area, then north into Napa and Sonoma counties, and south through the Peninsula to Santa Cruz and Monterey Bay, we found yarn shops big and small to fulfill all of your fiber wishes.

We hope you enjoy this fiber journey through the Bay Area—we can't wait to get back there ourselves.

Happy knitting!
Alice + Kathleen
Editors, One More Row Press

"The coldest winter I ever spent was a summer in San Francisco."
—NOT Mark Twain

Continuous

by Kelly White | Kelly White Designs

San Francisco artist, Ruth Asawa, created sculptures of individual, concentric, and overlapping spheres by bending wire into loops with her hands. Her spherical sculptures are rounded and strong, airy with distinct boundaries, and even though they are woven like baskets, they function only as art. Her sculptures are captivating. See page 12 for more on Ruth Asawa's work and life.

Continuous is a cocoon-shaped cardigan inspired by these sculptures. The lace rib body suggests Asawa's looping wires, while the rounded shape evokes spheres, and the ribbing echoes the structured edge. The body of the sweater is knit flat to start, then joined in the round at the ribbing. The cardigan requires only two short seams. Snug armholes and cuffs create the rounded, sculptural drape. The armholes are designed to have about 2 inches of negative ease around the widest part of the wearer's forearm, so it is important to consider forearm measurement when deciding which size to knit. The sweater is designed to have about 16 inches of positive ease at the bust. To get the fit you like best, you can work the body in one size and the armholes/cuffs in another.

Size
Adult XS (S, M, L, 1X, 2X, 3X)
Shown in size S with 14 inches/35.5 cm of positive ease

Materials
Sincere Sheep Favor (70% Merino, 30% Alpaca; Aran weight: 200 yd/183 m per 4 oz/113 g skein); color: Deepest Desire; 5 (5, 6, 6, 7, 8, 8) skeins or approx. 900 (1000, 1100, 1200, 1325, 1450, 1600) yds

US 9/5.5 mm 40-inch/100-cm circular needle, for body of sweater

US 7/4.5 mm 40-inch/100-cm circular needle, for ribbing

Two US 4, 5, or 6/3.5, 3.75, or 4 mm 36-inch/91-cm circular needle, for tubular bind off

Stitch marker, waste yarn, crochet hook (size I/9 or J/10), tapestry needle, a pin or clip (for seaming)

Gauge
15 sts x 16 rows = 4 inches/10 cm in Lace Rib stitch on largest needles, after blocking

Finished Measurements
Bust (horizontal distance between armholes): 43 ½ (48, 52, 56 ½, 61, 65, 69) inches/104 (110.5, 122, 143.5, 155, 165, 175) cm
Length (vertical distance between finished edges): 29 (30, 30, 31, 32, 33, 34) inches/73.5 (76, 76, 78.5, 81.5, 84, 86.5) cm
Armhole Circumference: 6 ½ (7, 7 ½, 8, 8 ½, 9 ½, 10 ½) inches/16.5 (18, 19, 20.5, 21.5, 24, 26.5) cm

Sincere Sheep

Through natural dyes, fiber, and crafting, Sincere Sheep connects to the past, other cultures, farmers, community, fiber mills, and to the land. Inspired by the concept of *terroir*, all yarn and fiber is dyed using color extracted from plants (and periodically from insects), responsibly sourced, some from locally-gathered leaves and flowers.

Sincere Sheep
Napa, CA
sinceresheep.com
@sinceresheep

Stitches

Lace Rib (worked flat)
Row 1 (WS): K1, (yo, k2tog, p1, k1) to end.
Row 2 (RS): P1, (yo, p2tog, k1, p1) to end.

Twisted Rib (worked in the rnd)
All Rnds: (K1-tbl, p1) to end.

Smocking Stitch (worked in the rnd)
Insert right hand ndl from front to back between specified sts on the left hand ndl.

Wrap the working yarn around the right hand ndl, as if to knit. Draw up a loop, and place the loop on the left hand ndl. Pull the loop moderately tight to gather the sts together. The fabric is very fluid, so the tighter smocking gives the opening more structure. Knit this loop together with the first st (k2tog).

Pattern

Body
With your largest circular ndl, CO 165 (181, 197, 213, 229, 245, 261) sts using Provisional CO (see Techniques, p. 62).

Work Lace Rib for 97 (101, 101, 105, 109, 113, 117) rows, or until piece measures 24 (25, 25, 26, 27, 28, 29) inches/61 (63.5, 63.5, 66, 68.5, 71, 73.5) cm, and you have completed a WS row.

Ribbing
Set Up: With RS facing you, transfer the sts you just worked to a circular ndl two sizes smaller than the ndl you used to work the body. Pick up the sts along your provisional CO and remove the waste yarn. You will now have 330 (362, 394, 426, 458, 490, 522) sts on your circular ndl, which you will knit in the rnd. Pl m to indicate BOR.

Set Up Rnd: (K1-tbl, p1) until 1 st before the provisional cast-on sts, k2tog-tbl (this will reinforce the join), p1. Continue working (k1-tbl, p1) until 1 st before the BOR. Move BOR m back 1 st, k2tog-tbl to reinforce the join.

You will how have (328, 360, 392, 424, 456, 488, 520) sts on your circular ndl.

Rnds 1–7: Work Twisted Rib.

Rnd 8: *Smocking Stitch—Insert right hand ndl from front to back between the seventh and eighth sts on the left hand ndl. Wrap yarn around ndl. Pull resulting loop onto ndl and knit together with first st. (P1, k1-tbl) 3 times, p1. Rep from * to end of rnd.

Rnds 9–10: Work Twisted Rib for 2 rnds.

Rnd 11: (K1-tbl, p1) twice, *Smocking Stitch—Insert right hand ndl from front to back between the seventh and eighth sts on the left hand ndl. Wrap yarn around ndl. Pull resulting loop onto ndl and knit together with first st. (P1, k1-tbl) 3 times, p1. Rep from * to 4 sts before end of rnd. Complete one more Smocking Stitch to pull together the last 4 sts of the rnd with the first 4 sts of the previous rnd.

Rnd 12: Work Twisted Rib.

Work Tubular BO (see Techniques).

Armholes and Cuffs
To make the armholes, find one of the two openings between the ribbing and the body of the sweater. Fold the body of the sweater so that right sides are facing each other, the ribbing is on the right, the edges of the ribbing are even with each, and the edges of the opening are even at the top. Measure 3 ¼ (3 ½, 3 ¾, 4, 4 ¼, 4 ¾, 5 ¼) inches/ 8 (9, 9.5, 10, 11, 12, 13.5) cm starting at the fold at the body of the sweater. Use a pin (or sewing clip) to mark that measured distance and attach both sides of the sweater together at that point. Take your tapestry needle, threaded with a length of yarn about 3 times as long as the seam you will sew, and beginning at the ribbing, use a backstitch technique to seam the edges of the body until you reach the pin marking the armhole. Cut yarn, leaving a 6-inch/15-cm tail.

Set Up Rnd: Using the same circular ndl you used for the ribbing on the body of the sweater, pick up and knit 26 (28, 30, 32, 34, 38, 42) sts around the armhole. Pl m to indicate BOR.

Rnds 1–30: Work Twisted Rib.

Work Tubular BO. Cut yarn, leaving a 6-inch/ 15-cm tail.

Rep for second armhole and cuff.

Finishing
Weave in all ends, invisibly, on the wrong side of the fabric.

Soak in lukewarm water with wool wash for ten minutes. Rinse and squeeze out water. Lay flat to dry, patting smooth to finished measurements. Because the sweater is circular, the fabric will dry with creases at the edges unless you shift the sweater to reposition the creases as the piece dries. But any creases can be easily removed later with steam from an iron.

Kelly loves San Francisco

What has your knitwear design journey been like?
My knitwear design journey has been full of knowledgeable, thoughtful local businesswomen who see the value in supporting our community—knitting and otherwise. I am so fortunate to have connected with them.

Tell us about a special San Francisco place...
The **Presidio Nursery** is a magical portal into the world of local ecology, native plants, volunteering, and community building.

Favorites to knit to?
I can knit and listen, but aside for stolen glances up, I can't really watch or read while I knit. Audiobooks and podcasts, though, work great for me. I'll listen to any book that Bahni Turpin or Cherise Boothe record. I loved *Children of Blood and Bone* by Toni Adyemi and *An Unkindness of Ghosts* by Rivers Solomon.

BART/MUNI knitting: must-have or never ever? Project monogamy or cast on all the things?
I usually bring knitting with me when there's a chance I'll be waiting for public transit—MUNI especially. But let's be honest, I almost always have a project with me just in case I have a few minutes I'm waiting around anywhere. I generally have no more than two or three projects going at one time.

Favorite place in San Francisco?
Immigrant Point Overlook when the whales are in town!

Ruth Asawa

Text & photos by Kelly White

Every time my son and I are in Union Square, we stop by Ruth Asawa's **San Francisco Fountain** to delight in the many little stories and neighborhood images it contains. In 1973, Asawa and over 250 participants between the ages of 3 and 90 created San Francisco in 41 panels that were ultimately cast in bronze and made to surround a circular pool.[1] The participants used baker's clay to shape the San Francisco scenes. When the owner of the new Hyatt Hotel expressed concern that the fountain would look like a giant cookie, Asawa agreed, and said, "That's what I want it to look like."[2] To represent the city on the fountain, they took a map and noted where the landmarks were in relation to the fountain. Asawa explained, "We started from the west side and worked our way along, the Golden Gate Park on the west, the financial district on the other side."[3] Asawa's mother, who was visiting from Southern California during this project, made many leaves for the trees on the sculpture.

It's safe to say that you could spend hours poring over the details of this fountain. We notice new things every time we stop, and we always leave feeling happy and connected to our community. These warm feelings are a testament to Asawa's genius and her approach to public art: "When you work out in the public, it's just not the place to express yourself. You need to do something that will allow the people who see it to respond to it."[4] It's truly amazing to see our present day city both reduced to and amplified by a fountain that was completed more than 40 years ago.

Asawa's inclusive approach to the fountain's creation was absolutely intentional. As she explained,

> Since we have no real folk art or craft tradition any more in this country, this kind of activity has to be recreated to bring families and communities together. … When the [Hyatt] fountain came along I thought it was a great opportunity to show how group skills could be used to make something that people usually think of as high art—one product from one person's mind and hands. … It is the idea of bringing skills together that interests me. We see this in science, in the space program, but we have lost it in art.[5]

By the early 1970s, Asawa had become known locally for her public commissions. The commissions included the **San Francisco Fountain**, the **Andrea Fountain** in **Ghirardelli Square** ("a fantastical scene of two seated mermaids—one nursing an infant— surrounded by turtles, frogs, and lily pads") and two origami-inspired metal sculptures at **Buchanan Plaza** in **Japantown**.[6] She had, however, been creating and exhibiting her wire sculptures since the 1940s. Unfortunately, those sculptures were not always seen as art.

One of the people who truly appreciated from the beginning how Asawa brought her artistry to life was the 20th-century inventor and visionary Buckminster Fuller. In 1971, Fuller wrote a letter in support of Ruth Asawa's application to the Guggenheim Foundation's annual fellowship program. He noted that he had been writing candidates' recommendations for forty-three years, and he went on to say, "I state, without hesitation or reserve, that I consider Ruth Asawa to be the most gifted, productive, and originally inspired artist that I have ever known personally. That statement includes many of this century's most celebrated greats."[7] He specifically mentioned Asawa's wire sculptures, as well as her achievements in building a "fascinating and inspiring" home with her husband, raising a family, and bringing an innovative arts curriculum to San Francisco Public Schools.[8] The Foundation denied her application. While the Foundation could have simply overlooked Asawa, it seems far more likely that their denial was based on a distasteful cocktail of biases. As a woman of Japanese heritage who integrated her life and her work, creating sculptures at home with simple materials and craft techniques while raising six children, Ruth Asawa probably didn't look to the Foundation like "a true artist." She wasn't male, white, or aloof.

Ruth (Aiko) Asawa was born on January 24, 1926, in Norwalk, California, to parents who had emigrated to the United States from Japan. She was the fourth of seven children. The Asawas were farmers: her father, Umakichi, was an itinerant farm worker in Japan who came to the United States to make his fortune; her mother, Haru, came from Nobe, a village where they raised silkworms and spun silk. When Umakichi, came to California in 1914, the law forbade his becoming a citizen or owning land. He was, however, permitted to lease land. Once he had secured property, he began raising market basket crops. The whole family, including all the children, worked on the farm every day. Asawa and her siblings also attended Norwalk public school five days a week. On Saturdays, they could choose to work in the fields or attend Japanese language school. They always chose school.

Everything changed for the Asawas and more than 100,000 other Japanese Americans following the attack on Pearl Harbor in December 1941. In February 1942, around the time President Franklin D. Roosevelt issued Executive Order 9066 (which authorized the government to relocate and imprison people of Japanese ancestry on the West Coast in concentration camps), and without warning or explanation, FBI agents came and arrested Umakichi while he was eating lunch at home. They ransacked the house, and then took Umakichi away. The family didn't know where he was sent. In April 1942, Haru and the children were ordered to report to the Santa Anita Racetrack, euphemistically called an "assembly center." They each packed one small suitcase and left their house forever. They were put up in the horse stables, and the conditions were terrible:

> They whitewashed the stalls before we came in. You could see strands of hair between the cracks where the horses rubbed the boards. We were given two stalls. My brothers lived in one and we lived in the other. They gave us an army blanket, a pillow, and a cot. We made our own mattresses out of straw, and we had a kind of ticking for the cover.[9]

The Asawas spent as much time outside as they could because the stables stank of horse. They had a choice to go to school or to work; Haru chose work and the children chose school. A few Japanese artists from Disney Studios were imprisoned at Santa Anita, too, and Ruth began to take art classes from them.

After about six months, the government sent Haru and the children to Rohwer, Arkansas, one of ten permanent concentration camps. The children were allowed to go to school at Rohwer. Asawa took painting and drawing classes, in addition to required classes. She recounted that in a social studies class, the teacher made them say the "Pledge of Allegiance to the Flag" every day, and when they got to "with liberty and justice for all," they always added in a loud voice, "Except for us!" It made the teacher furious, but they did it anyway.[10] Asawa graduated from high school in 1943; although the war was not over, the government permitted her and other graduates a one-way ticket to any college in the Midwest (not the West Coast). Asawa chose the cheapest college, Milwaukee State Teachers College, planning to become an art teacher. After she completed three years of coursework, though, she learned no school would hire her because of her Japanese ancestry. She had to leave the school without graduating. She ultimately enrolled at Black Mountain College (BMC), and her experiences as a student there formed the springboard for her artistic career. BMC was also where she met Albert Lanier, the man who would become her husband.

In 1949, following their education at BMC, Asawa joined Lanier in San Francisco where he was working as an architectural draftsman. Over the next 60 years, Asawa continued to pursue her art career, Lanier his architecture career, and they both worked together to build a life and raise six children in San Francisco. "My materials were simple," said Asawa, "and whenever there was a free moment, I would sit down and do some work. Sculpture is like farming. If you just keep at it, you can get quite a lot done."[11]

Part of Asawa's legacy includes her vision for and commitment to introducing San Francisco public school students to art. She was one of the founders of the Alvarado Art Workshop, which brought meaningful art, artistic opportunities, and arts funding into schools. Asawa also served eight years on the San Francisco Art Commission, and was appointed to Jimmy Carter's Presidential Commission on Mental Health (serving on its Role of the Arts Committee). She was a member of the National Endowment for the Arts Task Force, and she served for two years at the request of Governor Jerry Brown on the California Arts Council. Asawa took art, artists, and advocacy seriously.[12]

You can see Asawa's wire sculptures today at the **de Young Museum** in San Francisco, as well as in other collections. Thanks to her impressive body of public work, everyone who spends time in San Francisco can also still bask in and be inspired by Asawa's creative, resilient, and generous spirit.

> "Sculpture is like farming. If you just keep at it, you can get quite a lot done."
> —Ruth Asawa

---

1   Bell, Tiffany. 2018. "Ruth Asawa: Working from Nothing." In *Ruth Asawa*. Edited by Anne Wehr, p. 12.
2   Hoefer, Jacqueline. 2006. "Ruth Asawa: A Working Life." In *The Sculpture of Ruth Asawa Contours in the Air*. Edited by Daniel Cornell, p. 26.
3   Ibid.
4   Bell, 12.
5   Ibid, 13.
6   Ibid, 12.
7   Ibid, 11.
8   Ibid.
9   Hoefer, 13.
10 Ibid.
11 Ibid, 19.
12 Ibid, 24.

Ferry Building

by Sloane Rosenthal | Hudson + West Co.

The Ferry Building pullover is a slightly-cropped, drop-shouldered pullover featuring a graphic cable motif around the bottom hem. Finished with ribbed sleeves and a dramatic cowl neck, the sweater has a modern, easy-to-wear silhouette that pairs well with pants and skirts alike. Short rows give the hem the slightest hint of a flattering, youthful, high-low curve.

The sweater is worked in pieces and seamed, with minimal shaping below the underarms. Increases along the armhole subtly angle the sleeves, while sloped bind-offs shape and anchor the shoulders. After the sweater is seamed, stitches are picked up from the neckline and the cowl neck is knit in the round.

Notes

- For casting on use the Long-Tail Cast-On or other stretchy cast-on method.
- Slip all stitches purlwise.
- Eliminating stitches on Rows 28, 32, and 36 of the chart reduces the number of stitches in each cable panel, and this is shown on the chart by the "no stitch" symbol. Simply proceed to the next square on the chart to continue working the cable panel.

Sizes

Adult XS (S, M, L, 1X, 2X, 3X)
Shown in size S with 9 ½ inches/24 cm positive ease

Materials

Hudson + West Co. WELD (70% U.S. Merino, 30% U.S. Corriedale; Fingering weight: 200 yd/183 m per 1.76 oz/50 g skein); color: Ash; 8 (8, 9, 10, 11, 11, 12) skeins or approx. 1450 (1575, 1700, 1900, 2025, 2200, 2300) yds

US 4/3.5 mm 32-inch/81-cm circular needle

US 3/3.25 mm 32-inch/81-cm circular needle, or one size smaller than gauge needle

For cowl, either one set of DPNs or long circular needle (for Magic Loop) in gauge needle, one and two sizes smaller, and one and two sizes larger

Tapestry needle, stitch markers, cable needle (optional)

Gauge

26 sts x 36 rows = 4 inches/10 cm in Stockinette stitch on larger needles, after blocking

Finished Measurements

Bust circumference: 41 ½ (45 ½, 49 ½, 54 ½, 58 ½, 62 ½, 66 ½) inches/104.5 (115.5, 126, 138.5, 148.5, 159, 169) cm
Sleeve length to underarm: 15 (15, 15, 15 ½, 15 ½, 15 ½, 16 ¼) inches/38 (38, 38, 39.5, 39.5, 39.5, 41.5) cm
Upper arm circumference: 9 ¾ (12 ¼, 12 ¼, 13, 14 ¼, 14 ¾, 16) inches/25 (31, 31, 33, 36, 37.5, 40.5) cm
Cuff circumference: 8 (8 ½, 8 ½, 8 ½, 9 ¼, 9 ¼, 9 ¼) inches/20.5 (21.5, 21.5, 21.5, 23.5, 23.5, 23.5) cm
Body length to underarm: 14 (14 ½, 14 ½, 14 ½, 15, 15, 15 ½) inches/35.5 (37, 37, 37, 38, 38, 39.5) cm
Cowl length: 12 inches/30.5 cm (all sizes)

Hudson + West Co.

Designer-driven and knitter-focused, Hudson + West sources and produces yarn from sheep to skein in the U.S. Founded in 2019, this bi-coastal company introduced a heathered blend of Corriedale and Merino wool in two 3-ply weights: Forge (worsted) and Weld (fingering) in an elegant palette of 13 colors with plans to expand.

Hudson + West Co.
New York, NY + San Francisco, CA
hudsonandwestco.com
@hudsonandwestco

Pattern

Front

Using smaller ndl CO 198 (214, 230, 262, 278, 294, 310) sts.

Ribbing Row 1 (RS): K1, *p2, k2, rep from * to last st, k1.

Ribbing Row 2 (WS): K1, work in est patts to last st, k1.

Work back and forth in est patts until piece measures approx 3 inches/7.5 cm from CO edge.

Switch to larger ndl.

Establish cable panel as follows:

For sizes XS (—, M, L, —, 2X, —) only:
Row 1 and all RS rows: K1, p2, work sts 1–32 of Ferry Building chart 6 (—, 7, 8, —, 9, —) times, k1.

Row 2 and all subsequent WS rows: K1, work in est patts to last st, k1.

For sizes — (S, —, —, 1X, —, 3X) only:
Row 1 and all RS rows: K1, p2, work sts 1–32 of chart — (6, —, —, 8, —, 9) times, work sts 1–16 of the Ferry Building chart once, p2, k1.

Row 2 and all subsequent WS rows: K1, work in est patts to last st, k1.

For all sizes:
Work all 36 rows of cable pattern as charted. Note that you will dec 36 (39, 42, 48, 51, 54, 57) sts as you resolve the cables in the chart—162 (175, 188, 214, 227, 240, 253) sts.

Establish Stockinette stitch as follows:

All subsequent RS rows: Knit all sts.

All subsequent WS rows: K1, purl to last st, k1.

Continue in Stockinette stitch until piece measures approx 14 (14, 14 ½, 14 ½, 15, 15, 15 ½) inches/35.5 (35.5, 37, 37, 38, 38, 39.5) cm from CO edge.

Armhole Shaping

Shaping Row (RS): K1, m1-R, cont as est to last st, m1-L, k1—2 sts inc'd; 164 (177, 190, 216, 229, 242, 255) sts.

Cont as est, working shaping row every 6 (6, 6, 8, 8, 8, 10) rows seven more times—14 sts inc'd; 178 (191, 204, 230, 243, 256, 269) sts.

Cont as est, working even until piece measures approx 5 (5 ½, 6, 6 ½, 7, 7 ½, 8) inches/12.5 (14, 15, 16.5, 18, 19, 20.5) cm from first inc row.

Neckline and Shoulder Shaping

Next row (RS): K77 (83, 88, 101, 107, 113, 119) sts, BO next 24 (25, 28, 28, 29, 30, 31) sts, knit to end.

Note: You will now work only the sts for the Right Shoulder and Neckline Shaping.

Next row (WS): K1, purl to last st, k1.

Neckline Dec Row 1 (RS): K1, ssk, knit to end—1 st dec'd; 76 (82, 87, 100, 106, 112, 118) sts.

Neckline Dec Row 2 (WS): K1, purl to last three sts, p2tog, k1—1 st dec'd; 75 (81, 86, 99, 105, 111, 117) sts.

Rep these two rows 2 more times—4 sts dec'd; 71 (77, 82, 95, 101, 107, 113) sts.

Shaping Row 1 (RS): K1, ssk, cont as est to last st, k1—70 (76, 81, 94, 100, 106, 112) sts.

Shaping Row 2 (WS): BO 5 (5, 5, 6, 7, 7, 7) sts, cont as est to last three sts, k1—65 (71, 76, 88, 93, 99, 105) sts.

Shaping Row 3: K1, ssk, cont as est to last st, sl1 wyib—64 (70, 75, 87, 92, 98, 104) sts.

Shaping Row 4: Sl2 wyif, slip 1st st over 2nd st (1 st BO'ed), BO 4 (4, 4, 5, 6, 6, 6) more sts, cont as est to last st, k1—59 (65, 70, 81, 85, 91, 97) sts.

Shaping Rows 5–12: Rep Shaping Rows 3&4 four more times—35 (41, 46, 53, 53, 59, 65) sts.

Shaping Row 13: K1, — (ssk, ssk, ssk, ssk, ssk, ssk), cont as est to last st, sl1 wyib—35 (40, 45, 52, 52, 58, 64) sts.

Shaping Row 14: Sl2 wyif, slip 1st st over 2nd st (1 st BO'ed), BO 3 (4, 4, 5, 5, 6, 6) more sts, cont as est to last st, k1—31 (35, 40, 46, 46, 51, 57) sts.

Shaping Row 15: K1, — (—, ssk, ssk, ssk, ssk, ssk), cont as est to last st, sl1 wyib—31 (35, 39, 45, 45, 50, 56) sts.

Shaping Row 16: Sl2 wyif, slip 1st st over 2nd st (1 st BO'ed), BO 3 (4, 4, 5, 5, 5, 6) more sts, cont as est to last st, k1—27 (30, 34, 39, 39, 44, 49) sts.

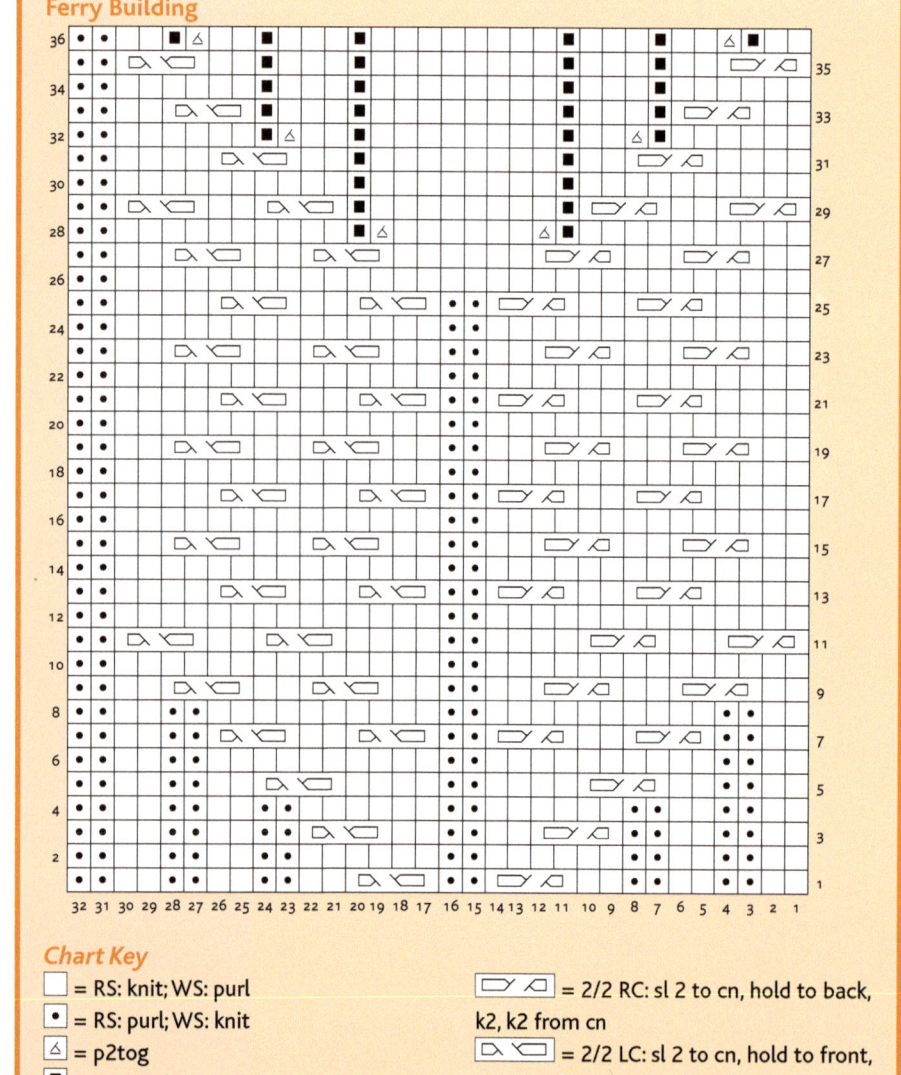

Ferry Building

Chart Key

☐ = RS: knit; WS: purl
• = RS: purl; WS: knit
△ = p2tog
■ = no stitch

⟋⟍ = 2/2 RC: sl 2 to cn, hold to back, k2, k2 from cn

⟍⟋ = 2/2 LC: sl 2 to cn, hold to front, k2, k2 from cn

Shaping Row 17: K1, — (—, —, —, —, ssk, ssk), cont as est to last st, sl1 wyib [27 (30, 34, 39, 39, 43, 48) sts.

Shaping Row 18: Sl2 wyif, slip 1st st over 2nd st (1 st BO'ed), BO 3 (4, 4, 5, 5, 5, 6) more sts, cont as est to last st, k1—23 (25, 29, 33, 33, 37, 41) sts.

Shaping Rows 19–20: Rep Shaping Rows 17&18—19 (20, 24, 27, 27, 30, 33) sts.

Shaping Row 21 and all remaining RS rows: Knit to last st, sl1wyib.

Shaping Row 22: Sl2 wyif, slip 1st st over 2nd st (1 st BO'ed), BO 3 (3, 4, 5, 5, 5, 6) more sts, cont as est to last st, k1—15 (16, 19, 21, 21, 24, 26) sts.

Shaping Row 24: Sl2 wyif, slip 1st st over 2nd st (1 st BO'ed), BO 3 (3, 4, 5, 5, 5, 6) more sts, cont as est to last st, k1—11 (12, 14, 15, 15, 18, 19) sts.

Shaping Row 26: Sl2 wyif, slip 1st st over 2nd st (1 st BO'ed), BO 3 (3, 4, 4, 4, 5, 6) more sts, cont as est to last st, k1—7 (8, 9, 10, 10, 12, 12) sts.

Shaping Row 28: Sl2 wyif, slip 1st st over 2nd st (1 st BO'ed), BO 3 (3, 4, 4, 4, 5, 5) more sts, cont as est to last st, k1—3 (4, 4, 5, 5, 6, 6) sts.

Shaping Row 30: BO all remaining sts.

Reattach yarn to WS of sweater at outer edge of Left Neckline. You will now work only the sts for the Left Shoulder and Neckline.

Neckline Dec Row 1 (RS): K1, knit to last three sts, k2tog, k1—1 st dec'd; 76 (82, 87, 100, 106, 112, 118) sts.

Neckline Dec Row 2 (WS): K1, p2tog, purl to last st, k1—1 st dec'd (81, 86, 99, 105, 111, 117) sts.

Rep these two rows 2 more times—4 sts dec'd; 71 (77, 82, 95, 101, 107, 113) sts.

Shaping Row 1 (RS): BO 5 (5, 5, 6, 7, 7, 7) sts, cont as est to last three sts, k1; 66 (72, 77, 89, 94, 100, 106) sts on ndl.

Shaping Row 2 (WS): K1, p2tog, cont as est to last st, sl1 wyif—65 (71, 76, 88, 93, 99, 105) sts.

Shaping Row 3: Sl2 wyif, slip 1st st over 2nd st (1 st BO'ed), BO 4 (4, 4, 5, 6, 6, 6) more sts, cont as est to last st, k1—60 (66, 71, 82, 86, 92, 98) sts.

Shaping Row 4: K1, p2tog, cont as est to last st, sl1 wyif—59 (65, 70, 81, 85, 91, 97)) sts.

Shaping Rows 5–12: Rep Shaping Rows 3&4 four more times—35 (41, 46, 53, 53, 59, 65) sts.

Shaping Row 13: Sl2 wyib, slip 1st st over 2nd st (1 st BO'ed), BO 3 (4, 4, 5, 5, 6, 6) more sts,

cont as est to last st, k1—31 (36, 41, 47, 47, 52, 58) sts.

Shaping Row 14: K1, — (p2tog, p2tog, p2tog, p2tog, p2tog, p2tog), cont as est to last st, sl1 wyif—31 (35, 40, 46, 46, 51, 57) sts.

Shaping Row 15: Sl2 wyib, slip 1st st over 2nd st (1 st BO'ed), BO 3 (4, 4, 5, 5, 5, 6) more sts, cont as est to last st, k1—27 (30, 35, 40, 40, 45, 50) sts.

Shaping Row 16: K1, — (—, p2tog, p2tog, p2tog, p2tog, p2tog), cont as est to last st, sl1wyif—27 (30, 34, 39, 39, 44, 49) sts.

Shaping Row 17: Sl2 wyif, slip 1st st over 2nd st (1 st BO'ed), BO 3 (4, 4, 5, 5, 5, 6) more sts, cont as est to last st, k1—23 (25, 29, 33, 33, 38, 42) sts.

Shaping Row 18: K1, — (—, —, —, —, p2tog, p2tog), cont as est to last st, sl1 wyif—23 (25, 29, 33, 33, 37, 41) sts.

Shaping Rows 19–20: Rep Shaping Rows 17&18—19 (20, 24, 27, 27, 30, 33) sts.

Shaping Row 21: Sl2 wyif, slip 1st st over 2nd st (1 st BO'ed), BO3 (3, 4, 5, 5, 5, 6) more sts, cont as est to last st, k1—15 (16, 19, 21, 21, 24, 26) sts.

Shaping Row 22 and all remaining WS rows: K1, purl to last st, sl1 wyif.

Shaping Row 23: Sl2 wyif, slip 1st st over 2nd st (1 st BO'ed), BO 3 (4, 5, 5, 5, 5, 6) more sts, cont as est to last st, k1—11 (12, 14, 15, 15, 18, 19) sts.

Shaping Row 25: Sl2 wyif, slip 1st st over 2nd st (1 st BO'ed), BO 3 (3, 4, 4, 4, 5, 6) more sts, cont as est to last st, k1—7 (8, 9, 10, 10, 12, 12) sts.

Shaping Row 27: Sl2 wyif, slip 1st st over 2nd st (1 st BO'ed), BO 3 (3, 4, 4, 4, 5, 5) more sts, cont as est to last st, k1—3 (4, 4, 5, 5, 6, 6) sts.

Shaping Row 29: BO all remaining sts.

Back

With smaller ndl CO 198 (214, 230, 262, 278, 294, 310) sts.

Ribbing Row 1 (RS): K1, *p2, k2, rep from * to last st, k1.

Ribbing Row 2 (WS): K1, work in est patts to last st, k1.

Work back and forth in est patts until piece measures approx 3 inches/7.5 cm from CO edge.

Switch to larger ndl.

Establish cable panel as follows:

For sizes XS (—, M, L, —, 2X, —) only:
Row 1 and all RS rows: K1, p2, work sts 1–32 of Ferry Building chart 6 (—, 7, 8, —, 9, —) times, k1.

Row 2 and all subsequent WS rows: K1, work in est patts to last st, k1.

For sizes — (S, —, —, 1X, —, 3X) only:
Row 1 and all RS rows: K1, p2, work sts 17–32 of Ferry Building chart once, then work sts 1–32 of chart — (6, —, —, 8, —, 9) times, K3.

17

Row 2 and all subsequent WS rows: K1, work in est patts to last st, k1.

For all sizes:
Work all 36 rows of cable pattern as charted. Note that you will dec 36 (39, 42, 48, 51, 54, 57) sts as you resolve the cables in the chart—162 (175, 188, 214, 227, 240, 253) sts.

Establish Stockinette stitch as follows:
All subsequent RS rows: Knit all sts.

All subsequent WS rows: K1, purl to last st, k1.

Work these two rows one more time, then work short rows as follows:

Short Row 1 (RS): Cont as est to 6 sts from end of row, w&t.

Short Row 2 (WS): Cont as est to 6 sts from end of row, w&t.

Short Row 3: Cont as est to 6 sts before previous wrapped st, w&t.

Short Row 4: Cont as est to 6 sts before previous wrapped st, w&t.

Short Rows 5–10: Rep Short Rows 3&4 three more times.

Next row (RS): Knit across row, resolving wraps as you come to them.

Next row (WS): Purl across row to last st, resolving wraps as you come to them, k1.

After conclusion of short rows, cont as est in stockinette until piece measures approx. 14 (14, 14 ½, 14 ½, 15, 15, 15 ½) inches/35.5 (35.5, 37, 37, 38, 38, 39.5) cm from CO edge.

Technique tip: you will need to measure at the edge of the piece, not the center, due to the short row shaping.

Armhole Shaping
Shaping Row (RS): K1, m1-R, cont as est to last st, m1-L, k1—2 sts inc'd; 164 (177, 190, 216, 229, 242, 255) sts.

Cont as est, working shaping row every 6 (6, 6, 8, 8, 8, 10) rows seven more times—14 sts inc'd; 178 (191, 204, 230, 243, 256, 269) sts.

Cont as est, working even until piece measures approx. 5 (5 ½, 6, 6 ½, 7, 7 ½, 8) inches/12.5 (14, 15, 16.5, 18, 19, 20.5) cm from first inc row.

Shoulder and Back Neck Shaping
Work six rows even.

Next row (RS): BO 5 (5, 5, 6, 7, 7, 7) sts, cont as est to last st, k1—173 (186, 199, 224, 236, 249, 262) sts on ndl.

Next row (WS): BO 5 (5, 5, 6, 7, 7, 7) sts, cont as est to last st, sl1 wyif—168 (181, 194, 218, 229, 242, 255) sts.

Shaping Row 3: Sl2 wyib, sl 1st st over 2nd st, BO 4 (4, 4, 5, 6, 6, 6) more sts, cont as est to last st, sl1 wyib—163 (176, 189, 212, 222, 235, 248) sts.

Shaping Row 4: Sl2 wyif, sl 1st st over 2nd st, BO 4 (4, 4, 5, 6, 6, 6) more sts, cont as est to last st, sl1 wyif—158 (171, 184, 206, 215, 228, 241) sts.

Shaping Rows 5–12: Rep Shaping Rows 3&4 four more times—118 (131, 144, 158, 159, 172, 185) sts.

Shaping Row 13: Sl2 wyib, sl 1st st over 2nd st, BO 3 (4, 4, 5, 5, 6, 6) more sts, cont as est to last st, sl1 wyib—114 (126, 139, 152, 153, 165, 178) sts.

Shaping Row 14: Sl2 wyif, sl 1st st over 2nd st, BO 3 (4, 4, 5, 5, 6, 6) more sts, cont as est to last st, sl1 wyif—110 (121, 134, 146, 147, 158, 171) sts.

Shaping Row 15: Sl2 wyib, sl 1st st over 2nd st, BO 3 (4, 4, 5, 5, 6, 6) more sts, cont as est to last st, sl1 wyib—106 (116, 129, 140, 141, 152, 164) sts.

Shaping Row 16: Sl2 wyif, sl 1st st over 2nd st, BO 3 (4, 4, 5, 5, 6, 6) more sts, cont as est to last st, sl1 wyif—102 (111, 124, 134, 135, 146, 157) sts.

Shaping Rows 17–20: Rep Shaping Rows 15&16 two more times—86 (91, 104, 110, 111, 122, 129) sts.

Shaping Row 21: Sl2 wyib, sl 1st st over 2nd st, BO 3 (3, 4, 5, 5, 5, 6) more sts, cont as est to last st, sl1 wyib—82 (87, 99, 104, 105, 116, 122) sts.

Shaping Row 22: Sl2 wyif, sl 1st st over 2nd st, BO 3 (3, 4, 5, 5, 5, 6) more sts, cont as est to last st, sl1 wyif—78 (83, 94, 98, 99, 110, 115) sts.

Shaping Rows 23–24: Rep Shaping Rows 21&22—70 (75, 84, 86, 87, 98, 101) sts.

Shaping Row 25: Sl2 wyib, sl 1st st over 2nd st, BO 3 (3, 4, 4, 4, 5, 6) more sts, cont as est to last st, sl1 wyib—66 (71, 79, 81, 82, 92, 94) sts.

Shaping Row 26: Sl2 wyif, sl 1st st over 2nd st, BO 3 (3, 4, 4, 4, 5, 6) more sts, cont as est to last st, sl1 wyif—62 (67, 74, 76, 77, 86, 87) sts.

Shaping Row 27: Sl2 wyib, sl 1st st over 2nd st, BO 3 (3, 4, 4, 4, 5, 5) more sts, cont as est to last st, sl1 wyib—36 (37, 45, 45, 51, 52) sts.

Shaping Row 28: Sl2 wyif, sl 1st st over 2nd st, BO 3 (3, 4, 4, 4, 5, 5) more sts, cont as est to last st, sl1 wyif—54 (59, 64, 66, 67, 74, 75) sts.

Shaping Row 29: Sl2 wyib, sl 1st st over 2nd st, BO 2 (3, 3, 4, 4, 5, 5) more sts, cont as est to last st, sl1 wyib—51 (55, 60, 61, 62, 68, 69) sts.

Shaping Row 30: Sl2 wyif, sl 1st st over 2nd st, BO 2 (3, 3, 4, 4, 5, 5) more sts, cont as est to last st, sl1 wyif—48 (51, 56, 56, 57, 62, 63) sts.

Next Row: BO all remaining sts.

Sleeve (make two)
Using smaller ndl CO 54 (54, 58, 58, 62, 62) sts.

Ribbing Row 1 (RS): K1, *k2, p2, rep from * to last st, k1.

Ribbing Row 2 (WS): K1, work in est patts to last st, k1.

Rep these two rows thirteen more times.

Inc row (RS): K1, m1-R, cont as est to last st, m1-L, k1—2 sts inc'd; 56 (56, 60, 60, 64, 64) sts.

Rep Inc row every 20 (10, 8, 8, 6, 6, 4) rows 5 (9, 11, 13, 15, 17, 21) more times—10 (18, 22, 26, 30, 34, 42) sts inc'd; 66 (74, 82, 86, 94, 98, 106) sts.

Work even until piece measures approx 15 (15, 15, 15 ½, 15 ½, 15 ½, 16 ¼) inches/38 (38, 38, 39.5, 39.5, 39.5, 41.5) cm from CO edge, ending after a WS row.

Next row (RS): BO all sts loosely.

Finishing
Soak in lukewarm water with Dawn (or similar soap) for ten minutes. Rinse and squeeze out water. Lay flat to dry, patting smooth to finished measurements. Seam sweater, beginning by seaming shoulders together, then seaming sleeves to body and then by sewing underarm and side seams.

Cowl
With RS facing, reattach yarn to WS of right side of back neck. Using ndl one size smaller than ribbing ndl, pick up and knit 1 st in every bound off st and 1 st in every row along each curved edge. Precise number of sts picked up does not matter, so long as it is a multiple of four.

Ribbing Rnd: *K2, p2; rep from * to end of rnd.

Rep Ribbing Rnd four times.

Switch to needle one size larger, and cont as est. Inc needle sizes every 2–3 inches/5–7.5 cm, until piece measures approx 12 inches/ 30.5 cm from neckline.

BO using your preferred stretchy BO method.

Weave in all ends. I recommend a final wet blocking to "set" the sweater before wearing.

Sloane loves San Francisco

What has your knitwear design journey been like?

I started knitting shortly after my daughter was born, when I desperately needed something to do with my hands. I was still practicing law full time, and because I had less time to make than I did time to think about all the things I wanted to make, I spent a lot of time thinking about the kinds of sweaters I wanted to knit, and all the modifications I wanted to do to sweaters that were close-but-not-quite to what I had in mind. I started working on my first designs in the spring of 2016, and my first book, *Independent Fabrication*, came out that fall. Over time, what started as a significant side-hustle became more and more of a hustle-hustle, and I left my law firm in 2018, with a plan to do both more design work and more teaching and writing. I partnered up with Meghan Babin, who had been a great friend since she first bought a sweater from me for *Interweave Knits*, to found Hudson + West Co. in late 2018, and we've spent most of 2019 working on both expanding my independent design work and getting Hudson + West ready to launch.

Tell us a San Francisco story…

I see a lot of "Valley famous" people who seem really well known around here, but probably no one who lived more than 50 miles away could pick out of a lineup (which is not, it turns out, very different from living in Washington). But, we were out at dinner a few weeks ago and my son, who is five, saw that a baby had dropped a toy out of his high chair, and picked the toy up and went to hand it to his father … who turned out to be Sergey Brin (one of the founders of Google).

BART knitting: must-have or never ever? Picker or thrower? Project monogamy or cast on all the things?

I don't do a ton of BART knitting (I was a huge DC Metro knitter), though I do a ton more car-knitting now that we live out here. I'm a picker, and almost always a monogamous knitter.

Top Ten TV shows (in no particular order):

Game of Thrones • The West Wing • Buffy the Vampire Slayer • The Americans • The Wire • The Good Wife • Luther • ER • Broadchurch • Bones

Favorite places to eat in SF?

The Progress, **State Bird Provisions**, **Trestle**, **Cotogna**.

Favorite place to be/walk/knit in the area?

Fort Funston. I love the ocean views, I love being in nature so close to the heart of the city, I love the way the wind off the coast warps the pine trees. We've been here for four years now, but the novelty of all the ways this area is physically different from our East Coast home still hasn't worn off. My favorite off-the-beaten track spot is in the south end of the Sonoma Valley: the **San Pablo Bay National Wildlife Refuge**. The drive there from the city is gorgeous—over the **Golden Gate Bridge** and up through **West Marin** and into the vineyards as you get towards **Petaluma**—but the refuge itself is super peaceful and calm, and you can see the boats on the water in one direction and vineyard views in the other. It's such a special spot, and having it be so close to the city is great.

Fog City

by Faina Goberstein

This two-color, somewhat slouchy hat is knit in the round from bottom up to the crown. Stripes and two slip-stitch patterns combine to achieve the look of a foggy day in the city. Colors are chosen to show in slip-stitch patterns and to convey the feel of the fog when it covers half of the landscape, including the bridges of San Francisco.

Notes

- Work the Long-Tail Cast-On holding CC on your thumb and MC on your index finger to achieve the edge in CC.
- All stitches are slipped purlwise.
- The float tension must be a little looser than for knitting a stitch.
- If you are not using the yarn, carry it up the back at the beginning of rnd.
- It is helpful to place markers after each rep of the pattern and later at the crown decrease to separate sections.
- wyb = with yarn in back

Size

Adult S (M, L, XL)
Shown in size M

Materials

Sincere Sheep Covet DK (60% Wool, 25% Alpaca, 15% Silk; DK weight: 150 yd/ 137 m per 1.98 oz/56 g skein);
  MC: Bare Grey; 1 (1, 2, 2) skeins
  CC: Cumulus; 1 skein for all sizes

US 6/4.0 mm 16-inch/41-cm circular needle

US 4/3.5 mm 16-inch/41-cm circular needle, or needle two sizes smaller than gauge needle

Tapestry needle, stitch markers

Gauge

20 sts x 28 rnds = 4 inches/10 cm in Stockinette stitch on larger needle, after blocking

Finished Measurements

To fit a circumference at band: 19 (20, 21, 22) inches/49 (51, 53.5, 56) cm
Depth: 9 ½ inches/24 cm

Sincere Sheep

Through natural dyes, fiber, and crafting, Sincere Sheep connects to the past, other cultures, farmers, community, fiber mills, and to the land. Inspired by the concept of *terroir*, all yarn and fiber is dyed using color extracted from plants (and periodically from insects), responsibly sourced, some from locally-gathered leaves and flowers.

Sincere Sheep
Napa, CA
sinceresheep.com
@sinceresheep

Pattern

Brim
With both CC and MC and Long-Tail Cast-On (see Notes), using smaller ndl, CO 86 (90, 96, 100) sts. Pl m for BOR and join for working in the rnd, being careful not to twist sts.

Rnds 1–7: With MC, (k1, p1) around. Carry CC up the back.

Body
With MC and larger ndl, knit one rnd and inc 6 (2, 6, 2) sts using m1-L inc evenly spaced—92 (92, 104, 104) sts.

With CC, knit one rnd and purl one rnd.

With MC knit four rnds.

Work 10 rnds of Slip-Stitch Dashes.

With MC, knit one rnd.

With MC, knit one rnd and inc 8 (8, 6, 6) sts using m1-L inc—100 (100, 110, 110).

With MC, knit one rnd.

With CC, knit one rnd and purl one rnd.

With MC, knit one rnd.

Work 30 rnds of Slip-Stitch Diamonds and Stripes.

With MC, knit four rnds.

Break CC.

For sizes S (M) only:
Next rnd: *K23, k2tog; rep from * to end of rnd—96 (96) sts.

For sizes L (XL) only:
Next rnd: (K12, k2tog) six times, (k11, k2tog) twice—102 (102) sts.

Crown Shaping
Next rnd: *K14 (14, 15, 15), k2tog, pl m; rep from * four more times, k14 (14, 15, 15), k2tog—90 (90, 96, 96) sts.

Knit one rnd.

Dec rnd: *Knit to 2 sts before m, k2tog; rep from * to end of rnd—6 sts dec'd.

Knit one rnd.

Rep last two rnds until there are 4 sts in each of 6 sections—24 sts.

Finishing
Break MC, leaving a 10-inch/25-cm tail. Thread tail onto tapestry needle and slip all remaining sts onto tapestry needle, then pull tail to close up top of hat. Weave in all ends. Soak in lukewarm water with wool wash for ten minutes. Rinse and squeeze out water. Lay flat to dry, patting smooth to finished measurements.

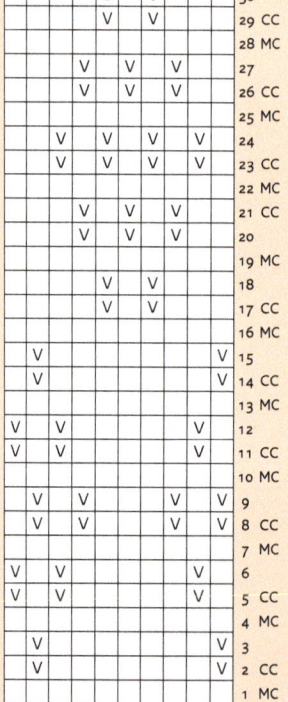

Slip-Stitch Dashes

Chart Key
- ☐ = knit
- • = purl
- V = sl p-wise wyb

Slip-Stitch Dashes

Rnds 1 & 9: With CC, *K2, sl2 wyb; rep from * to end of rnd.

Rnds 2 & 10: *P2, sl2 wyb; rep from * to end of rnd.

Rnds 3 & 4: With MC, knit to end of rnd.

Rnd 5: With CC,* sl2 wyb, k2; rep from * to end of rnd.

Rnd 6: *Sl2 wyb, p2; rep from * to end of rnd.

Rnds 7 & 8: With MC, knit to end of rnd.

Slip-Stitch Diamonds And Stripes

Rnds 1, 4, 7, 10, 13, 16, 19, 22, 25, 28: With MC, knit to end of rnd.

Rnds 2, 3, 14 & 15: With CC, *sl1 wyb, k7, sl1 wyb, k1; rep from * to end of rnd.

Rnds 5, 6, 11 & 12: With CC, *k1, sl1 wyb, k5, sl1 wyb, k1, sl1 wyb; rep from * to end of rnd.

Rnds 8 & 9: With CC, *sl1 wyb, k1, sl1 wyb, k3, (sl1 wyb, k1) twice; rep from * to end of rnd.

Rnds 17, 18, 29 & 30: With CC, *k3, (sl1 wyb, k1) twice, k3; rep from * to end of rnd.

Rnds 20, 21, 26 & 27: With CC, *k2, (sl1 wyb, k1) three times, k2; rep from * to end of rnd.

Rnds 23 & 24: With CC, *k1, (sl1 wyb, k1) four times, k1; rep from * to end of rnd.

Faina loves San Francisco

What has your knitwear design journey been like?
Too long for a short answer :) I was taught how to knit socks at eight years old by my neighbor while living in Russia. Since that evening, I have had needles and yarn in my hands almost every day. It helped me with all kinds of happenings throughout my life. I was always interested in many knitting and crochet techniques. While I was building my career as a math professor, I was also attending a two-year professional knitting design course to get a deeper understanding of body types and flat-pattern making. Since 2004, I publish my designs in magazines, books, etc.

As a designer, I am very interested in texture and how to apply it to a flattering, well-fitted garment.

Tell us a San Francisco story...
There are many celebrities who either live here or come to visit. You could dine in a restaurant and see that at the next table sits Adrian Grenier (*Devil Wears Prada*) with his friend.

One story though stands out for me the most: My daughter and my granddaughter were strolling in their Laurel Heights neighborhood and went in to a store where Diane Keaton was signing her new book on interior design.

BART knitting: must-have or never ever? Favorite neighborhood? Picker or thrower? Project monogamy or cast on all the things?
I use BART occasionally and always have my knitting with me there. SF neighborhoods: **Laurel Heights**, **Presidio**, **Noe Valley**, and **Berkeley**. I am a continental knitter but teach both. I knit and crochet all things but like to design garments.

Favorite places to eat, drink, and knit in SF?
I am a snob about good food and have many places I love in the city, but the one that I frequent in San Francisco is **Nopalito** (organic Mexican hot spot). In Berkeley I love **Corso**, **Pedro's Brazil Cafe**, and **Musashi**.

I love to knit at the ocean or bay in the city, and the Rose Garden in Berkeley.

Grant Avenue Stroll

by Yvonne Poon | Gamer Babe Knits

Born and raised in San Francisco, I spent a lot of my childhood in Chinatown, and this wrap highlights some of my favorite places. Begin at Dragon's Gate, the gateway to Chinatown, then look up as you head north: lanterns as far as the eye can see. I loved going to the Chinese New Year parade as a child, anticipating the long, colorful dragon at the end. To celebrate Chinese New Year, as well as birthdays, weddings, red egg and ginger parties, and many other holidays, we would go to Four Seas Restaurant, owned for over 25 years by my uncle, aunt, and cousins—can you see the gold chandeliers with lotus blossoms in the banquet room? To finish, on the northern outskirts of Chinatown, was Jec's Sewing Shop, owned by my mom, filled with the lively chatter of the seamstresses (my "aunties") sewing, the clicking of the buttonhole machine, and the rhythmic hum of the sewing and overlock machines. And, of course, the cable car (my favorite, even now!), which runs along the western edge of Chinatown. Take a stroll with me along Grant Avenue, the heart of Chinatown.

Grant Avenue Stroll is a curved, textured wrap to keep you warm in the cold San Francisco weather (or cold weather anywhere). Five different stitch patterns, worked from south to north, with cables worked at the same time on the western edge will keep your needles knitting and interest high. Garter sections are worked in between each stitch pattern. Integrated i-cords finish the western and eastern edges of the wrap. The curved shape (for easier wearability) is achieved with short rows. There is never a dull moment as you stroll through and knit San Francisco's Chinatown through my needles.

Notes

- Instructions for this wrap are given in sections. The row counts given in each section are for that section only, not cumulatively for the whole wrap.
- The German short row method is used to create the curved shape of the wrap. Short rows are the result of turning your work before reaching the end of the row. Work to the turning point as indicated, then turn. Slip the stitch purlwise with yarn in front, pulling the yarn up and over the needle creating a double stitch. Continue working the row as instructed. When working the double stitch on the next row, knit or purl the stitch as one stitch, then continue working the row.
- Sections 2, 3, 4 & 5 will most likely be narrower than section 1 as you are working. Block these sections to the same approximate width as section 1.

Size
One size

Materials
The Dye Project Montara DK (100% Corriedale; DK weight: 260 yd/238 m per 3.5 oz/100 g skein); color: Dragon Breath; 4 skeins

US 6/4.0 mm 24-inch/60-cm circular needle

Cable needle, 1 stitch marker, tapestry needle, stitch markers in a second color (optional, for marking reps in Section 3)

Gauge
21 sts x 31 rows = 4 inches/10 cm in Stockinette stitch, after blocking

The Dye Project

Born out of a desire to combine the gorgeous colors and variations of hand dyed processes with wooly non-superwash yarn that people will love to knit, all of The Dye Project's yarns have been carefully chosen to be both wonderful to work with and fabulous to wear. They do require a bit of extra care by hand washing only, but they're totally worth it.

The Dye Project
Santa Cruz, CA
thedyeproject.com
@thedyeproject

Finished Measurements
Wingspan/Length (top edge): 59 inches/150 cm
Wingspan/Length (bottom edge): 76 inches/193 cm
Depth/Width (ends): 16 inches/41 cm
Depth/Width (center): 13 inches/33 cm

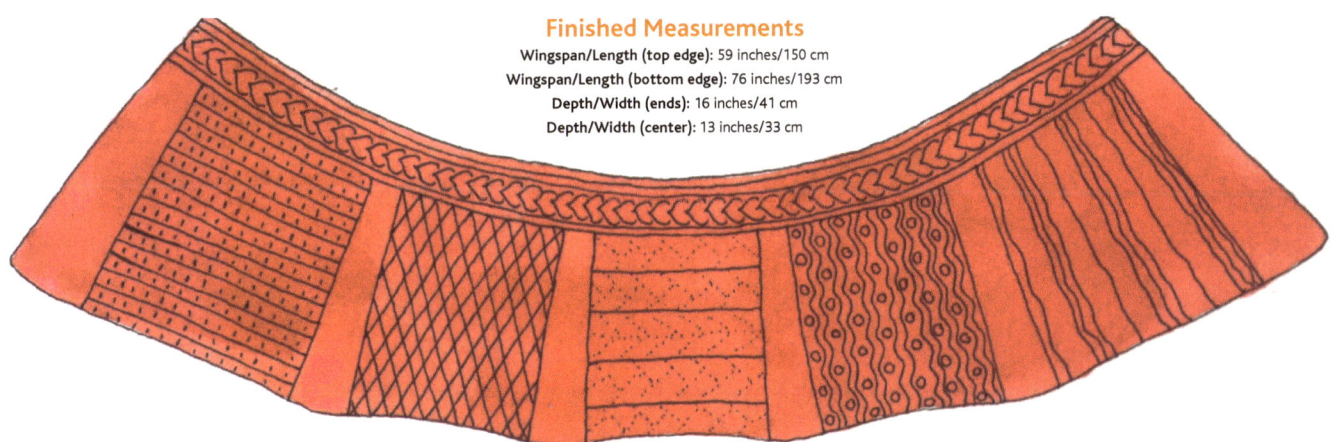

Pattern
CO 81 sts.

Bottom Edge
Rows 1 & 3 (RS): Knit.

Row 2 (WS): Sl2 p-wise wyif, knit to last 2 sts, sl2 p-wise wyif.

Row 4: Sl2 p-wise wyif, k17, pl m, knit to last 2 sts, sl2 p-wise wyif.

Row 5: Knit to m, sl m, p2, 1/1 RC, p2, k2, p1, k2, p2, 1/1 LC, p2, k2.

Row 6: Sl2 p-wise wyif, k2, p2, k2, m1-Rp, p1, m1-Lp, p1, k1, p1, m1-Rp, p1, m1-Lp, k2, p2, k2, sl m, knit to last 2 sts, sl2 p-wise wyif—4 sts inc'd, 85 sts.

Short Row Section A
Row 1 (RS): Knit to m, sl m, work row 1 of Cable Car Tracks.

Row 2 (WS): Work row 2 of Cable Car Tracks, sl m, knit to last 2 sts, sl2 p-wise wyif.

Rows 3 & 15 (short row): K32, turn.

Rows 4, 6, 8, 12, 14 & 16 (short row): Sl1 p-wise wyif, bring the working yarn up and over the top of the RH ndl, knit to last 2 sts, sl2 p-wise wyif.

Rows 5 & 13 (short row): K47, turn.

Rows 7 & 11 (short row): Knit to m, turn.

Row 9: Knit to m, sl m, work Row 3 of Cable Car Tracks.

Row 10: Work Row 4 of Cable Car Tracks, sl m, knit to last 2 sts, sl2 p-wise wyif.

Row 17: Knit to m, sl m, work Row 5 of Cable Car Tracks.

Row 18: Work Row 6 of Cable Car Tracks, sl m, knit to last 2 sts, sl2 p-wise wyif.

Section 1 – Dragon's Gate
Continue working Cable Car Tracks over last 23 sts on Rows 3–8 of Dragon's Gate.

Rows 1–104: Work Dragon's Gate Rows 1–8 thirteen times total.

Row 105 (short row) (RS): Work Row 1 once more.

Row 106 (short row) (WS): Sl1 p-wise wyif, bring the working yarn up and over the top of the RH ndl, knit to last 2 sts, sl2 p-wise wyif.

Short Row Section B
Row 1 (RS): Knit to m, sl m, work Row 1 of Cable Car Tracks

Row 2 (WS): Work Row 2 of Cable Car Tracks, sl m, knit to last 2 sts, sl2 p-wise wyif.

Rows 3 & 19 (short row): K17, turn.

Rows 4, 6, 8, 10, 14, 16, 18 & 20 (short row): Sl1 p-wise wyif, bring the working yarn up and over the top of the RH ndl, knit to last 2 sts, sl2 p-wise wyif.

Rows 5 & 17 (short row): K32, turn.

Rows 7 & 15 (short row): K47, turn.

Rows 9 & 13 (short row): Knit to m, turn.

Row 11: Knit to m, sl m, work Row 3 of Cable Car Tracks.

Row 12: Work Row 4 of Cable Car Tracks, sl m, knit to last 2 sts, sl2 p-wise wyif.

Row 21: Knit to m, sl m, work Row 5 of Cable Car Tracks.

Row 22: Work Row 6 of Cable Car Tracks, sl m, knit to last 2 sts, sl2 p-wise wyif.

Section 2 – Lanterns
Continue working Cable Car Tracks over last 23 sts on Rows 3–8 of Lanterns.

Rows 1–10: Work Lanterns Rows 1–10 once.

Rows 11–106: Work Rows 3–10 twelve times.

Short Row Section C
Work as for Short Row Section B—22 rows.

Section 3 – Chinese New Year Parade
Continue working Cable Car Tracks over last 23 sts on Rows 3–8 of Chinese New Year Parade.

Rows 1–10: Work Chinese New Year Parade Rows 1–10 once.

Rows 11–66: Work Rows 3–10 seven times.

Rows 67–73: Work Rows 3–9 once more.

Row 74 (short row) (WS): Sl1 p-wise wyif, bring the working yarn up and over the top of the RH ndl, knit to last 2 sts, sl2 p-wise wyif.

Short Row Section D
Work as for Short Row Section B—22 rows.

Section 4 – Four Seas Restaurant
Note: One stitch is increased to work this section. At the end of this section, one stitch is decreased to restore the stitch count.

The yarn overs worked in this section on Rows 4 & 12 do not count as increased stitches, as they will be dropped on the subsequent rows (5 & 13).

The Set-up Row counts as the Row 1 of the first repeat of the Four Seas Restaurant stitch pattern. After working Set-up Row, begin working Four Seas Restaurant stitch pattern with Row 2.

Continue working Cable Car Tracks over last 23 sts on Rows 3–8 and 11–16 of Four Seas Restaurant.

Set-up row (short row) (RS): K3, m1-R, knit to m, turn—1 st inc'd; 86 sts.

Rows 2–16: Work Four Seas Restaurant Rows 2–16 once.

Rows 17–64: Work Rows 1–16 three times.

Rows 65–79: Work Rows 1–15 once more.

Row 80 (WS): Work Row 6 of Cable Car Tracks, sl m, knit to last 4 sts, k2tog, sl2 p-wise wyif—1 st dec'd; 85 sts.

Short Row Section E

Work as for Short Row Section B—22 rows.

Section 5 – Jec's Sewing Shop

Continue working Cable Car Tracks over last 23 sts on Rows 3–8 and 11–16 of Jec's Sewing Shop.

Rows 1–18: Work Jec's Sewing Shop Rows 1–18 once.

Rows 19–82: Work Rows 3–18 four times.

Rows 83–88: Work Rows 3–8 once more.

Short Row Section F

Work as for Short Row Section A—18 rows.

Top Edge

Row 1 (short row) (RS): Knit to m, turn.

Row 2 (short row) (WS): Sl1 p-wise wyif, bring the working yarn up and over the top of the RH ndl, knit to last 2 sts, sl2 p-wise wyif.

Row 3: Knit to m, sl m, p2, 1/1 RC, p2, ssk, k2tog, p1, ssk, k2tog, p2, 1/1 LC, p2, k2—4 sts dec'd, 81 sts.

Rows 4 & 6: Sl2 p-wise wyif, knit to last 2 sts, sl2 p-wise wyif.

Row 5: Knit all sts.

BO all sts loosely. Break yarn leaving a 6-inch/15-cm tail.

Finishing

Weave in all ends. Soak in lukewarm water with wool wash for ten minutes. Rinse and squeeze out water. Lay flat to dry, pinning out to finished measurements.

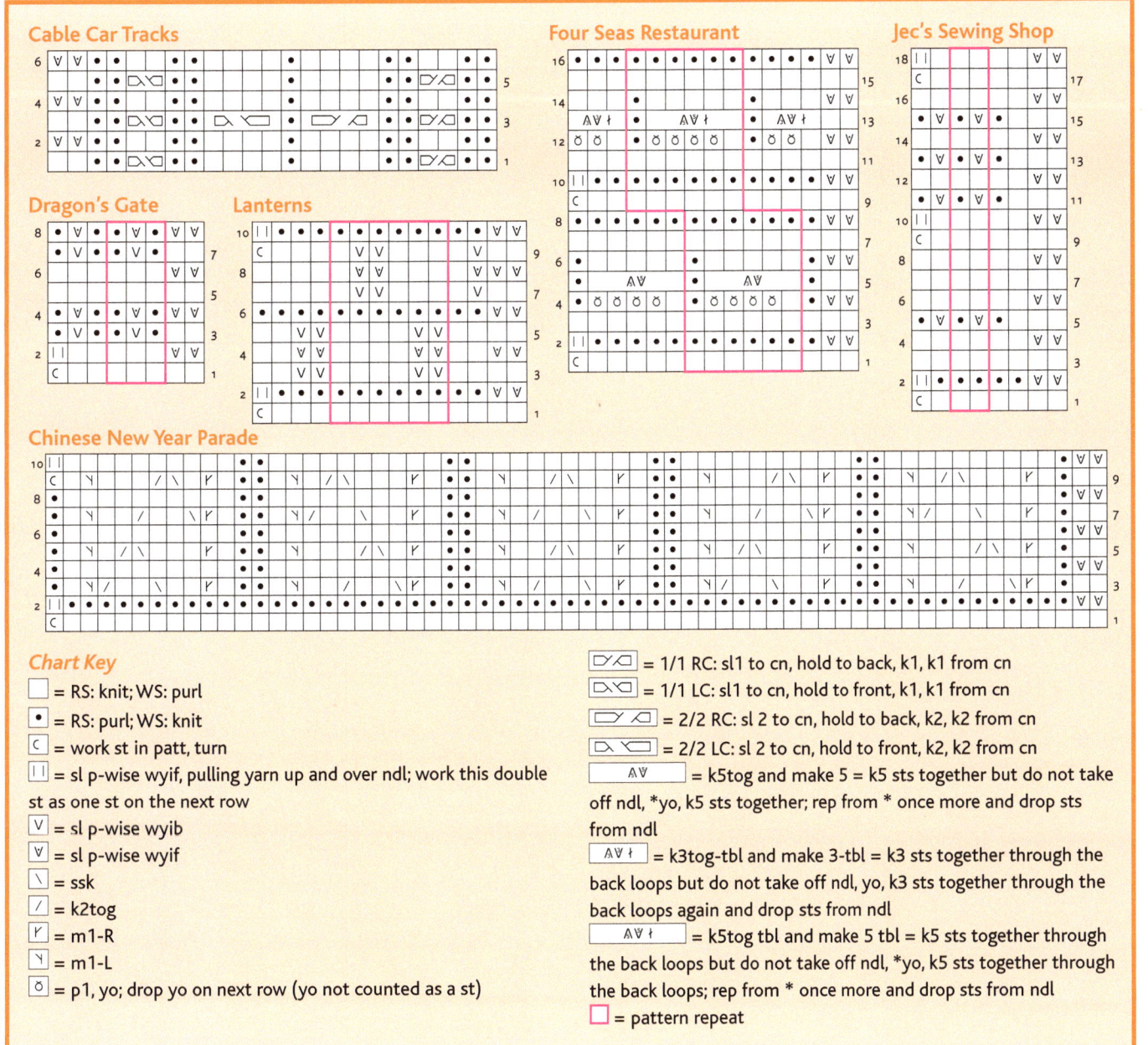

Yvonne loves San Francisco

Tell us a San Francisco story…

When my kids were little, we took them on a cable car ride for the first time. We started on Powell and Market and admired different parts of the city along the way. We got off at Lombard Street to explore that crooked street, then we hopped back on to finish the ride to **Ghirardelli Square**. We played tourist and walked around the Square, **Aquatic Park**, and **Fisherman's Wharf**. It was a gorgeous day in the city. When we were done, we took the cable car back to **Union Square** and stopped at **Lefty O'Doul's** for a late lunch. We had our old favorites: pastrami sandwiches and tapioca pudding. It was one of the best days ever.

BART/MUNI knitting: must-have or never ever? Picker or thrower? Project monogamy or cast on all the things? Favorite neighborhood?

I knit on BART and MUNI if I get a seat. Thrower, but can pick. Cast on all the things!!! Neighborhood: **Chinatown** because it's where I feel at home. We used to go shopping in Chinatown every Saturday, bringing home fresh fruits, vegetables, meat, fish, and dim sum. Once in awhile we got to bring home Botan rice candy and haw flakes as a treat. When my grandmother wanted to go to Chinatown, I would go with her because that meant I could ride the cable car!

Favorite places to knit and eat in San Francisco?

Knit: **Oracle Park** while watching baseball.
Eat: Some of my favorite places are no longer open. Some are still around, and thankfully there are some new places:

- **Capital** on Clay for the fried chicken wings!
- **East Ocean Seafood** in Alameda was owned by my aunt's family for over 25 years. They sold the restaurant in early 2019, and the food is still delicious. My favorite is crispy chicken stuffed with sticky rice, and their dim sum is outstanding.
- **Eastern Bakery** on Grant—I'm not a sweets person, but I love the coffee crunch cake. One of the few desserts I will never turn down.
- **Fenton's** in Oakland—I know, I just said I'm not a sweets person. We hung out here a lot when I was in college at UC Berkeley. We had many spoon tests because their sundaes were huge!
- **Giorgio's** on Clement and 3rd for the best mushroom pizza!
- **Golden Star Vietnamese** in Chinatown—when I worked in the Financial District, my coworkers and I would come here almost every Friday to have pho.
- **Oracle Park**—loaded tater tots, garlic fries, and crab sandwiches. The tater tots are crispy even when they get cold!
- **Original Joe's** at Westlake—get the Joe's Special and the ravioli.
- **R&G Lounge** on Kearny—the Live Crab with Salt and Pepper is the best!
- **Udon Mugizo** in Japantown—I first had dipping udon in Hawaii. Now I can have dipping udon without having to go to Hawaii!

Kathleen loves San Francisco

Tell us your connection to San Francisco...

When I was a teen, my family visited the Bay Area a couple of times, and, despite the sour expression on my face in our classic boat-to-Alcatraz photos (the boat ride on the Bay and **Alcatraz** itself are fantastic experiences), I loved the whole area from Big Sur and Monterey Bay to San Francisco, all the way up the coast to Mendocino.

Once I was a grown-up with a job, I was lucky enough to attend a training course in Pacific Grove while working for an educational publisher, and I almost took a job with them. Later in my career I worked for another publisher with headquarters in Sonoma County and would visit occasionally to confer with my West Coast counterparts.

Much as I consider myself an East Coast gal, there is something special out west, particularly the quality of the light.

Favorite San Francisco Movies, Books, & TV Shows

The Crying of Lot 49 by Thomas Pynchon • *Dark Passage* (1947) • *High Anxiety* (1977) • *The Maltese Falcon* (1941) • *Return of the Jedi*—the Endor scenes were filmed in Redwood National Park (1983) • *So I Married an Axe Murderer* (1993) • *Tales of the City* series of books by Armisted Maupin • *Vertigo* (1958) • *We Bare Bears* on Cartoon Network • *Zodiac* (2007)

Favorite places to eat in the Bay Area?

I'm going to take you farther afield, since other designers have shared some great SF spots...

Starting waaaaay to the south, there is nothing like the burger at **Nepenthe**. OK, it's an hour south of Monterey in Big Sur, but if you've got the time, the food and the cliffside view are spectacular.

Thanks to Trish Richman of **@carpeyarn**, we met up with many of our designers and dyers at **Nick's Rockaway** in Pacifica (down the road from **The Royal Bee Yarn Company**). What more do you need to know than "Crab Cake Benedict"? It's one of those old-school places by the water that can accommodate a large group of enthusiastic fiber folks, as well as tourists, regulars, grown-ups, and little kids.

In San Francisco you have to go to **Swan Oyster Depot** for the raw bar—be sure to bring cash, prepare to queue, and only go for breakfast or lunch. For coffee and pastries in a light-filled space, Alice and I loved **Le Marais Bakery** catercorner from **ImagiKnit**, where we met up with Brit-Marie of **Love Fest Fibers**.

Up in Santa Rosa, **A'Roma Roasters** has been roasting coffee since 1991 and used to provide my caffeine fix when I would stay at **Hotel La Rose** (around the corner) on business. What a treat that they are still there and still serving up delicious coffee and snacks, as well as hosting live music on weekend evenings.

Over in Napa we went to an outpost of **Hog Island Oyster** at the **Oxbow Public Market**, where you can sit at the bar (under the old dory suspended from the ceiling) or out on the deck and devour delicious seafood. Not surprisingly they have a great wine selection, too.

View of Golden Gate Bridge back to SF

Alice loves San Francisco

Tell us your connection to San Francisco...

My grandparents lived outside Santa Cruz for most of my life and my connection to the Bay Area is definitely southern looking. Vacations would begin at the San Jose airport and the trip over the mountains on Hwy 17 is still something I find myself doing in dreams, oddly enough. Friends have moved in and out of the area through the years, always giving a good reason to visit, and now my brother lives in the city proper. To me, this part of California radiates the feeling of profound creativity from food to technology, architecture to literature, and of course, fiber arts.

Where to eat in San Francisco?

Kathleen and I both loved **Nopa** on Divisadero Street @ Hayes for upscale SF dinner. Reservations are notoriously hard to get, but we showed up early and were lucky enough to get a great table. Order lots of little plates, you won't be disappointed. We loved the Little Fried Fish, Roasted Carrots, Green Salad, and well ... everything really. The Warm Goat Cheese serves as a simple dessert and the cocktails were expertly mixed.

Things I wish I'd known...

SF hills are no joke. Wear sensible shoes. Also, traffic. My god.

View of the city from Mission Dolores Park

Half-Moon

by Julie Weisenberger | Cocoknits

I distinctly remember discovering Love Fest Fibers at West Coast Craft (a great SF market filled with local creatives selling their wares) a couple years ago. I was immediately smitten with the yarn, the process, the story—and, of course, the lovely people behind the company. I couldn't resist a few balls of Tough Love Tiny, and they lived, as decoration, in my workspace until finally one day, I decided what to do with them. I wanted to knit a rug and played around with the design—constantly simplifying because the yarn is a bit of a challenge to knit with! I finally came up with a deceptively simple-to-knit half moon (or gibbous) shape, and the tassels added the perfect fun finish. My original rug lives by my bedside, and I adore that the first thing my feet touch every morning is this gorgeous wool with such a wonderful story—the perfect way to start every day.

Note
Ordinarily when working short rows (this means working part way across a row, then turning and knitting back before completing the row), you would use a technique such as wrap and turn, or shadow wrap short rows. However, for this rug pattern, you can simply turn and work back—no wraps or holes to close!

Size
One Size

Materials
Rug: **Love Fest Fibers Tough Love Tiny** (100% New Zealand Wool; Jumbo weight: 25 yd/23 m per 7–9 oz/200–255 g ball); color: Maize; 4 balls

Tassels: **Cascade Ecological Wool** (100% Natural Peruvian Wool; Worsted weight: 478 yd/437 m per 8.82 oz/250 g skein); Color: 8095 Ebony; 1 skein (or worsted/aran weight yarn of your choice)

US 35/19 mm needles for working flat

Loome Slingshot XL tool (or a 3½-inch/9-cm wide card); DMC Embroidery Floss, color: dark brown (or color to match tassels) to attach tassels to rug; tapestry needle

Gauge
4 sts x 8 rows = 4 inches/10 cm in Garter stitch

Finished Measurements
Length: 32 inches/81 cm
Depth: 16 ½ inches/42 cm excluding tassels

Love Fest Fibers

With a thing for huge, cozy knits and a mission to incorporate fashion industry waste and recycled plastic bottle fiber into their yarns, Love Fest Fibers travels up and down the West Coast to source and spin the most beautiful fiber they can find. They also travel far, from Nepal to New Zealand, to partner with artisans and pastoralists to bring fiber to market with a story and the ability to support local livelihoods.

Love Fest Fibers
San Francisco, CA
lovefestfibers.com
@lovefestfibers

Pattern
Rug
With Rug yarn CO 17 sts.

Row 1 (RS): K15, turn (leaving 2 sts unworked).

Rows 2 (WS): K14, sl1 wyif.

Row 3: K13, turn (leaving 4 sts unworked).

Row 4: K12, sl1 wyif.

Row 5: K11, turn (leaving 6 sts unworked).

Row 6: K10, sl1 wyif.

Row 7: K9, turn (leaving 8 sts unworked).

Row 8: K8, sl1 wyif.

Row 9: K7, turn (leaving 10 sts unworked).

Row 10: K6, sl1 wyif.

Row 11: K5, turn (leaving 12 sts unworked).

Row 12: K4, sl1 wyif.

Row 13: K3, turn (leaving 14 sts unworked).

Row 14: K2, sl1 wyif.

Row 15: Knit all 17 sts.

Row 16: Sl1 wyif, put yarn to back and knit to last st, sl1 wyif.

Rep Rows 1–16 six more times. In the last rep, BO all 17 sts when working Row 16.

Tassels
With Tassel yarn make 9 tassels (see sidebar). Measure and mark for evenly-distributed tassel placement on outer curve of rug. Tie each tassel onto rug with embroidery floss.

Finishing
Work in yarn ends. I did not block this rug. Because the yarn is already felted, it didn't feel necessary. Be sure to use with an anti-slip rug underlay cut to size.

Making Tassels
This video from Loome will help you make a tassel: *https://www.youtube.com/watch?v=bdtLqTmqTZk* Or visit *theloome.com* to learn more.

1. Use the Loome Slingshot XL tool (or a card measuring approx. 3 ½ inches/9 cm).
2. Secure yarn to one side of the tool.
3. Wrap the yarn 60 revolutions around the tool for each tassel.
4. Secure yarn to the same side as in 2.
5. Follow the video instructions to finish the tassels, using the embroidery floss for the head knot and to attach the tassels to the rug.

Note: Tassels as shown on rug do not have a neck knot (mentioned in video).

Julie loves San Francisco

What has your knitwear design journey been like?
I learned to knit and completed my first sweater in college, while studying abroad in Salzburg, Austria. I was immediately smitten and have been knitting and designing ever since. In the 1980s I ran my own knitwear company; in the 1990s I designed sweaters for yarn companies and magazines; and in 2007 I founded *Cocoknits.com*, my pattern and tool company. Over the years I've worked on perfecting the top-down, seamless method of creating a set-in-sleeve sweater, which I call the Cocoknits Method for short. I have also developed a line of high-quality tools that make the process of knitting easier … and more delightful! It's been a crazy journey—I don't think I could have imagined where the path would lead when I started down it … I just took one step at a time in a direction that I hoped would inspire knitters, as well as keep my business viable.

Tell us a San Francisco story…
I would say the time I visited the **de Young Museum** and was taught by Ruth Asawa's granddaughter how to make the wire sculptures she is famous for. They look knitted but the construction is so novel and fascinating—and it was a complete honor to have been taught by Ruth's granddaughter. If you get a chance to see Ruth's work, hanging in the de Young Museum, it's a treat!

Favorite TV shows to knit to?
Pretty much anything playing on PBS—especially Henry Louis Gates, Jr. I love *Finding Your Roots* and *Reconstruction*. I also never miss Stephen Colbert, and other recent favorites (watched while knitting and in no particular order) include *Chewing Gum*, *Russian Doll*, *The Handmaid's Tale*, *Call the Midwife*, *Catastrophe*, *Project Runway*, and the remakes of *Vanity Fair*, *Howard's End*, and *The ABC Murders* … to name a few! Thank goodness there is so much to watch (and listen to) while knitting these days!

Favorite books?
A few of my favorite books in the past year are *The Book Thief*; *Sing Unburied, Sing*; *Song of Achilles*; and *White Fragility*. I'm currently reading the Patrick Melrose trilogy. I need to be better about listening to books while knitting, I don't read as much as I'd like!

BART knitting: must-have or never ever?
Because I knit so much at home, I'm more of a people-watcher or Kindle-reader on BART. That may also be because I don't take super frequent or long trips on BART, so don't feel like I need a project for the ride.

Favorite station?
My favorite station is **West Oakland**—because that means I've either just come up from under the Bay—or am headed down and under the water of the Bay—which is pretty mind-blowing if you think about it!

Picker or thrower?
I learned to knit in Austria, so I am a continental knitter. Does that make me a picker?

Project monogamy or cast on all the things?
All the things and then some. I find project bags IN my project bags. It's pretty out of control juggling all the yarns and ideas—in addition to the follow-up knitting that takes place while I'm writing a pattern. Never not knitting, for sure!

Favorite places to eat and drink in Oakland?
I'm an Oaklander, and we don't lack great food on this side of the Bay! A few favorites: Thai: **Daughter** or **Farmhouse Kitchen**. Italian: **Belotti**. Pizza: **Emilia's**. Mexican: **Cholita Linda** or **Comal**. Japanese: **Soba Ichi**, **Ippuku**, or **Ramen Shop**. Cambodian: **Nyum Bai**. Burmese: **Burma Superstar** or **Royal Rangoon**. Californian: **Oliveto**. Indian: **Viks** or **Dosa**.

I'm leaving out a bunch—but that's a start!

Lombard Street

by Audry Nicklin

Found in San Francisco, Lombard Street is one of the most crooked streets in the world. With eight hairpin turns, it was originally designed to allow cars to travel down the steep grade of the hill. The Lombard Street socks take you down a similar journey. Starting at the cuff, the cables twist and turn, eventually opening out at the toe.

When knitting these socks, keep in mind that the cabling across the top of the sock does not have as much stretch. If you have a favorite needle size to make socks with, consider going up one size.

Note
Kitchener Stitch
Bring tapestry needle through the first front stitch as if to purl, then through the first back stitch as if to knit, *through the first front stitch as if to knit and remove stitch from the knitting needle, then the next front stitch as if to purl, through the first back stitch as if to purl and remove stitch from knitting needle, then the next back st as if to knit; repeat from * to end.

Size
Women's S (M)
Shown in size S

Materials
Bay Street Yarns Ava (80% Superwash Merino Wool, 20% Nylon; Fingering weight: 400 yd/336 m per 3.53 oz/100 g skein); color: Garden Party; 1 (2) skeins

US 1/2.25 mm 32-inch/80-cm long circular needle (for working Magic Loop)

Stitch marker, cable needle, tapestry needle

Gauge
30 sts x 44 rows = 4 inches/10 cm in Stockinette stitch, after blocking

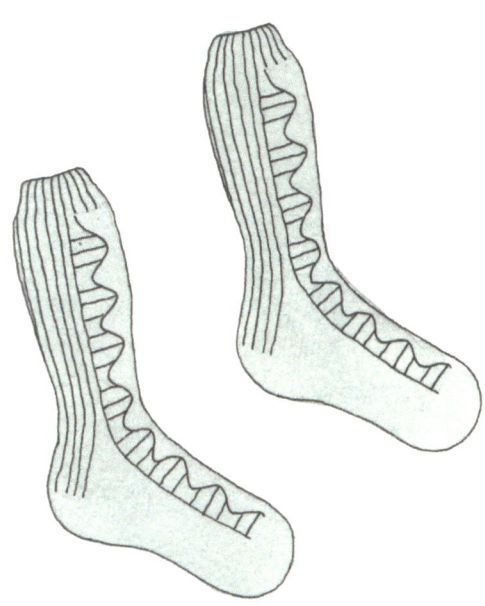

Finished Measurements
Foot circumference: 7 ¼ (8) inches/18.5 (20.5) cm
Leg length: 7 ½ inches/19 cm for both sizes

Bay Street Yarns

Dyeing yarn since 2016, when the business was called HKNT, Bay Street Yarns runs the gamut from luscious tonals to colorful variegated yarns. They offer a variety of bases from lace to bulky to choose from, plus dyed-to-order sweater quantities.

Bay Street Yarns
Northern California
baystreetyarns.com
@baystreetyarns

Pattern

Cuff
CO 64 (72) sts. Join for working in the rnd, being careful not to twist the sts, and pl m to indicate BOR.

If using the Magic Loop method, arrange the stitches so that there are 32 (36) sts on one side of the loop and 32 (36) sts on the other side of the loop.

For size S only:
Size S Rnd 1: (K1, p2, k1) to end.

For size M only:
Size M Rnd 1: (P1, k2, p1) to end.

For all sizes:
Work ribbing for 18 rnds total.

Leg
Rnd 1: Work the first 32 (36) sts on the ndls using Row 1 of Lombard Street chart. Work the remaining 32 (36) sts in est rib patt.

Rnd 2: Work the first 32 (36) sts on the ndls using the next row of chart. Work the remaining 32 (36) sts in est rib pattern.

Rep Rnd 2 until the chart has been worked 3 times through, then work Rows 1–15 once more—63 rows of chart worked.

Heel
For size S only:
Size S Row 1 (WS): Turn work. Sl1 p-wise wyif, (k2, p2) until 3 sts remain on the 2nd ndl, k2, p1—32 sts worked.

Size S Row 2 (RS): Turn work. Sl1 p-wise wyib, (p2, sl2 p-wise) until 3 sts remain on the 2nd ndl, p2, k1—32 sts worked.

For size M only:
Size M Row 1 (WS): Turn work. Sl1 p-wise wyif, (p2, k2) until 3 sts remain on the 2nd ndl, p3—36 sts worked.

Size M Row 2 (RS): Turn work. Sl1 p-wise wyib, k1, (sl1 p-wise, p2, sl1 p-wise) until 2 sts remain on the 2nd ndl, k2—36 sts worked.

For all sizes:
Rep Rows 1&2 for 2 ¼ inches/6 cm, or until desired heel length has been reached, ending after a RS row.

Heel Turn
Row 1: Turn work. With WS facing, sl1 wyif, p16 (18), p2tog, p1.

Row 2: Turn work. Sl1 wyib, k3, ssk, k1.

Row 3: Turn work. Sl1 wyif, purl until you are 1 st from previous gap, p2tog, p1.

Row 4: Turn work. Sl1 wyib, knit until you are 1 st from previous gap, ssk, k1.

Rep Rows 3&4 until all sts have been worked. There are 18 (20) heel sts remaining after completing the heel turn.

Gusset
Pick up and knit the slipped sts along side of heel. Pick up and knit one more st between the heel and the top of the sock. This is the new BOR.

Set-up Rnd: Work Row 16 of chart along the top 32 (36) sts of the sock. Pick up and knit one st between the top of the sock and the heel. Then pick up and knit the slipped sts along the side of the heel. Be sure the same number of sts have been picked up on both sides of the heel. Knit to end of rnd.

Rnd 1: Work the first 32 (36) sts using Row 1 of chart, ssk, knit to 2 sts from end, k2tog—2 sts dec'd.

Rnd 2: Work the first 32 (36) sts using the next row of chart, knit to end.

Rnd 3: Work the first 32 (36) sts using the next row of chart, ssk, knit to 2 sts from end, k2tog—2 sts dec'd.

Rep Rnds 2&3 until there are 64 (72) sts total. There will be 32 (36) stitches on the 1st ndl and 32 (36) stitches on the 2nd ndl.

Foot
Continue working the first 32 (36) sts using chart and knitting the remaining sts until the sock measures 1 ¼ (1 ¾) inches/3 (4.5) cm from the toe. Be sure to end on Rnd 1, 5, 9, or 13 of chart. If the foot isn't quite long enough after ending on one of these rnds, work a few rnds in Stockinette st until the correct length has been achieved.

Toe
Rnd 1: *K1, ssk, knit until three sts from end of 1st ndl, k2tog, k1. Rep from * once more—4 sts dec'd.

Rnd 2: Knit all sts.

Rep Rnds 1&2 seven (nine) times—18 sts remain on each ndl.

Finishing
Break yarn leaving a 24-inch/60-cm tail and thread onto tapestry needle. With 18 sts on 1st ndl and 18 sts on 2nd ndl, use the tapestry needle to graft the sts together using Kitchener Stitch (see Note). Weave in all ends. Soak in lukewarm water with wool wash for ten minutes. Rinse and squeeze out water. Lay flat to dry, patting smooth to finished measurements.

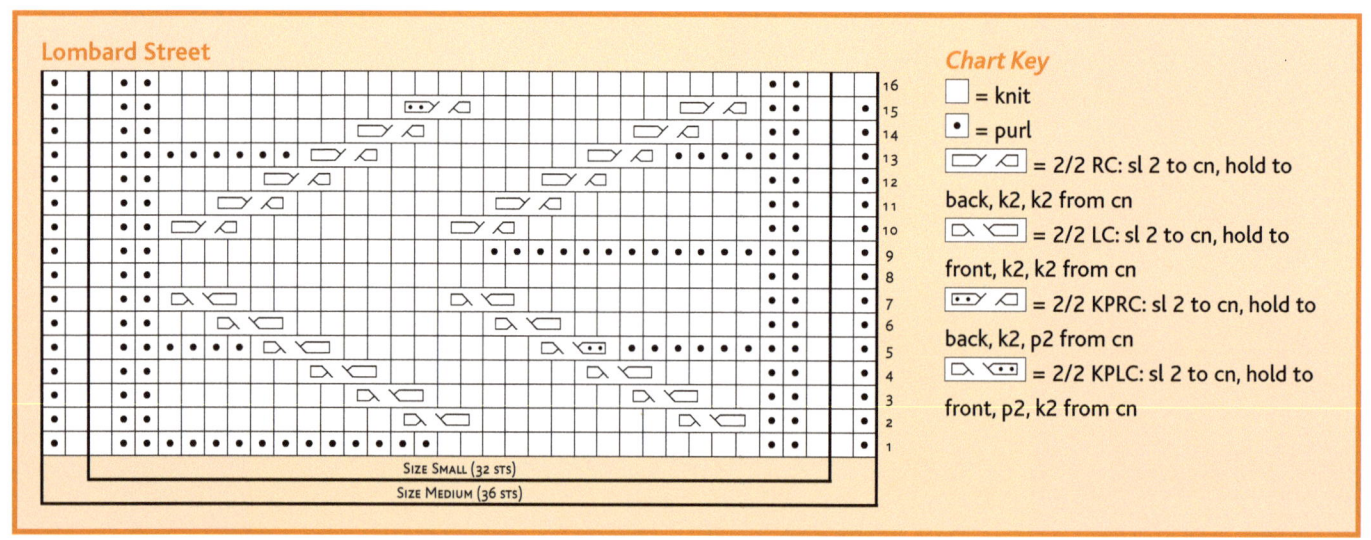

Audry loves San Francisco

What has your knitwear design journey been like?

I started knitting on a whim in high school. There weren't too many resources around, so I got a copy of *Knitting for Dummies*. With a little help from my Dad, who had knit in his childhood, I was off. It didn't take me long to start taking commissions for knitted items.

In college, around Halloween, I lost out on an Ebay auction for a Sherlock Holmes hat. Rather than be Sherlock Holmes, I decided to be a giraffe after finding a giraffe print sweater at the local thrift store. All I needed was a hat. I ended up designing and knitting one up. It didn't take long for me to start designing other animal hat patterns. A few years in to designing I was lucky enough to have a pattern accepted by *Twist Collective*: **Celestarium**.

Tell us a San Francisco story...

One of my favorite San Francisco memories is when a friend and I put our bikes in her car, drove up to San Francisco, and biked from the **Ferry Building**, across the **Golden Gate Bridge**, and all the way to **Sausalito**. We had lunch before taking the ferry back to the Ferry Building. It was a tough ride because of the strong headwind, but that lunch tasted amazing after all that exercise.

Top Ten favorite knits?

Determined by the number of times I've knitted it or how often I wear the knit:

- **Arrowhead Cardigan** by Anna Cohen
- **Seadragonus** by Wei Siew Leong
- **Sleepy Hollow Socks** by Lori Law
- **Pente** by Carol Feller
- **Primavera Socks** by Natalja
- **Haleakala** by Cookie A
- **Vanilla Latte Socks** by Virginia Rose-Jeanes
- **Iceland** by Stephanie White
- **Denature** by Margaret Mills
- **Lambing Mitts** by Veronika Jobe (Actually, my husband knit these for me, but I love wearing them.)

What are your favorite SF things to do?

My favorite place to be in San Francisco is **Golden Gate Park**. It is possible to rent bikes, or even rent a paddle boat. There is a **Japanese Garden**, a conservatory, and in the right season, the **Dahlia Garden** is full of blooms. Whenever I find myself in **Golden Gate Park**, I consider it a good day, if I can get a bottle of Strawberry Mint Refresca from one of the many cart vendors, and if I get to see a turtle in **Stow Lake**.

What is your favorite place to eat in SF?

This little place on Jackson Street called **Delicious Dim Sum**. It's the kind of place that if you blink, you'll miss it. But the food ... it is glorious!

Mission Dolores

by Heatherly Walker | Yarn Yenta

Inspired by the elaborately decorated entrance to the Mission Dolores Basilica, the twisted and cabled stitches of the Mission Dolores mittens add texture and interest to this traditional, bottom-up mitten pattern.

While the Mission itself was founded in 1776 as the Mission San Francisco de Asís (named for Saint Francis of Assisi), it quickly became known as Mission Dolores for a nearby creek. The present Mission Chapel is an adobe structure with a unique sanctuary mural, both created by Ohlone labor from 1788–1791. The Chapel is the oldest intact building in the city of San Francisco, having survived the 1906 earthquake and subsequent fires. Ostensibly built to convert the Indigenous people of Alta (Upper) California, the Mission devastated the Ohlone culture and population.

Adjacent to the Chapel, the Basilica was built after the earthquake. The Spanish Baroque ornamentation of the front entrance was added later, inspired by the Churrigueresque Revival of the Panama-California Exposition in 1926. This style of expressive decoration was popular in Spain in the late 17th century.

Note

If you cast on too tightly, consider the German Twisted Cast-On (also known as the Old Norwegian Cast-On). While similar to a Long-Tail Cast-On, it adds an extra twist to the finished cast-on to make it stretchier.

1. Make a slip knot and place it on one knitting needle.
2. Holding the yarn and needle in the right hand, pinch your left forefinger and thumb together and place in between the two strands hanging down from the needle, being careful not to twist the strands. Make sure that the tail is closest to you and draped over your thumb.
3. Grip the working yarn and tail together using the other fingers on your left hand.
4. Open up your forefinger and thumb and pull the needle down, exactly as if you are doing a Long-Tail Cast-On.
5. Using the tip of the right-hand needle, go under both sides of the loop wrapped around your thumb, hook the far side of the loop over the top with the tip of the needle and pull it toward you going under the side of the loop nearest you.
6. Then, with the tip of the needle reach over the top and catch the strand coming from your index finger over the top. You will notice that the loop around your thumb makes sort of a figure 8. Pull the strand you've just caught through the top of the figure 8 and drop the entire loop off your thumb.
7. Repeat for the number of stitches needed.

Sizes

Women's S (M, L)
Shown in size S

Materials

Speckled Finch Studios Bouncy DK (100% Merino Wool; DK weight: 231 yds/211 m per 3.5 oz/100 g skein); color: Amber; 1 skein for all sizes

US 2.5/3 mm set of DPNs

Stitch markers, waste yarn, tapestry needle

Gauge

28 sts x 40 rnds = 4 inches/10 cm in Stockinette stitch, after blocking

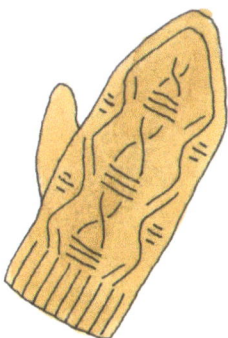

Finished Measurements
Hand circumference: 7 (7 ½, 8) inches/18 (19, 20) cm
Hand length: 9 ¼ (10, 10 ¾) inches/23.5 (25.5, 27.25) cm length

Speckled Finch Studios

Playing with color in knitting led to Speckled Finch Studios diving into the dyepot. Every skein is created with a lot of love and care. A variety of techniques are used to get specific colorways. One of the beauties of hand-dyed yarn is that each skein will be slightly different.

Speckled Finch Studios
Northern California
speckledfinchstudios.com
@speckledfinchstudios

Pattern

Cuff

CO 52 (55, 58) sts. Join for working in the rnd, being careful not to twist, and pl m to indicate BOR.

Ribbing Set-up Rnd: *(K1-tbl, p2) 8 (8, 9) times, k1-tbl, p1, pl side m, (k1-tbl, p2) 8 (9, 9) times, k1-tbl, p1.

Work in est ribbing for 12 (14, 16) rnds. Remove side m.

Hand

Left Mitten Set-up Rnd: K26 (27, 29), pl thumb1 m, k1, pl thumb2 m, k0 (1, 2), pl chart1 m, work Mission Dolores chart set-up rnd outlined in blue across 25 sts, pl chart2 m, k0 (1, 1).

Note: For Size Small chart1 marker is the same as thumb2, and chart2 marker is the same as the BOR marker.

Right Mitten Set-up Rnd: K26 (27, 29), pl chart1 m, work Mission Dolores chart set-up rnd outlined in blue across 25 sts, pl chart2 m, k0 (2, 1), pl thumb1 m, k1, pl thumb2 m, k0 (0, 2).

Note: For Size Small chart2 and thumb1 markers are the same. For Sizes Small and Medium, the BOR marker also serves as thumb2 marker.

Work in est patts 10 rnds total, working all sts outside of chart in Stockinette Stitch.

Thumb Gusset Rnd: Work to thumb1 m, sl thumb1 m, m1-l, k1, m1-r, sl thumb2 m, work

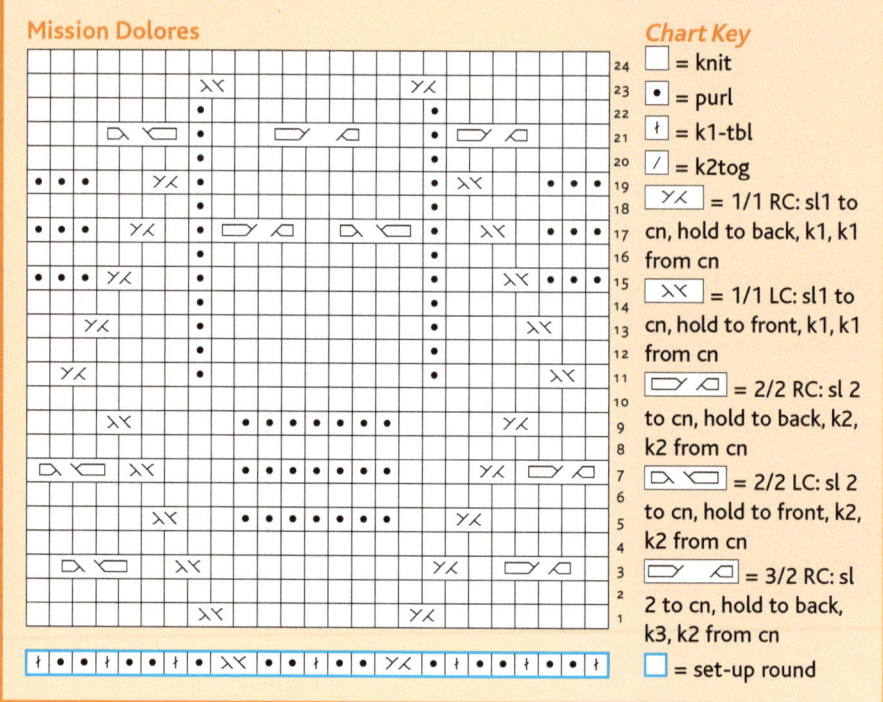

to end—2 sts inc'd.

Work one rnd in est patts.

Rep these two rnds 7 (7, 8) times total—15 (15, 19) sts between thumb ms.

Set Aside Thumb Rnd: Work in est patts to thumb1 m, remove thumb1 m, sl 15 (15, 19) sts to waste yarn, remove thumb2 m, m1-l, work in est patts to end—52 (55, 58) sts on needle, 15 (15, 19) sts on waste yarn.
Note: Continue to use chart and BOR markers.

Work in est patts 58 (62, 66) rnds total from Mitten Set-up Rnd or approx 1 ½ inches less than desired length of mitten.

Top

Continue working chart as long as there are sufficient stitches.

Top Dec Rnd: Ssk, k22 (25, 25), k2tog, k1, ssk, work chart to last three sts of rnd, k2tog, k1—4 sts dec'd.

Work one rnd in est patts.

Rep these two rnds 10 times total, knitting four fewer sts every Top Dec Rnd—12 (15, 18) sts.

For size S only:
Size S Dec Rnd: K2tog, k3, ssk, knit to end—10 sts.

For size M only:
Size M Dec Rnd: K2tog, knit to end—14 sts.

For size L only:
Size L Dec Rnd 1: K2tog, k7, ssk; k1, k2tog, k5, ssk, k1—14 sts.

Knit one rnd.

Size L Dec Rnd 2: K2tog, k5, ssk; k1, k2tog, k3, ssk, k1—10 sts.

For all sizes:
Break yarn leaving a 20-inch/50-cm tail and thread onto tapestry needle. Using Kitchener Stitch (see p. 35), graft together top of mitten.

Thumb

Slip 15 (15, 19) sts from waste yarn and distribute evenly onto three DPNs. Pl m to indicate BOR, join in working yarn, and knit all sts, then pick up and knit 3 sts from hand—18 (18, 22) sts.

Adjustment Rnd: K2tog, knit to last 3 sts, ssk, k1—16 (16, 20) sts.

Knit all rnds until thumb measures 1 ½ (1 ¾, 2) inches/3.75 (4.5, 5) cm.

Thumb Dec Rnd 1: (K2, k2tog) four (four, five) times—12 (12, 15) sts.

Knit one rnd.

Thumb Dec Rnd 2: (K1, k2tog) four (four, five) times—8 (8, 10) sts.

Break yarn leaving a 6-inch/15-cm tail and thread onto tapestry needle. Pull tail through live sts on ndl and cinch to close.

Finishing

Weave in all ends. Soak mittens in lukewarm water with wool wash for ten minutes. Rinse and squeeze out water. Lay flat to dry, patting mittens smooth to finished measurements.

Heatherly loves Paradise (& SF)

Tell us your Paradise story...

With six small children, there was a suggestion to take up a hobby to de-stress. I chose knitting and learned from Debbie Stoller's *Stitch N Bitch* book, then proceeded to read every knitting book in the public library. Within 6 months of first casting on, I was teaching at the new local yarn shop.

My husband began working with youth on the Ridge. I taught many of the kids to knit to help them cope with the stress of their lives. It calmed their ADD/ADHD for studying. Instead of dropping out, all of them graduated high school. They began approaching me for spare knitting needles. Those requests grew into a swap at Stitches West where individuals traded in old needles for raffle tickets to win yarn-y gift baskets.

I taught teenage girls to make baby booties for their friends and for their own babies. Our rough looking, over-6ft-tall boys would enter the LYS in search of pink and black yarns, so I could help them make hats while we drove to beaches, volcanic parks, or concerts with mosh pits. "Teach me how to..." opened many conversations and became an excuse to come over and crash on the bed the Walker family had under the steps in the living room for wayward souls.

Friends often joked that if you lived in Paradise and you knit, then "You must know Heatherly." WWKIP days were hosted at Terry Ashe Park. We spun and knit with Girl Scout troops, at the Silver Dollar Fairgrounds, at Patrick Ranch's annual Threshing Bee. Brooke and I formed the Paradise Knitters and Spinners Guild which met weekly at Feather River Gracious Retirement Center in Paradise for eight years. Residents would sit with us and share their stories, bring us projects for help, and have a Show & Tell of things they created once upon a time. Many dear friendships were formed there, giving the Walker girls many surrogate grandparents.

Through the encouragement of the Guild, I began designing and publishing. I would not be a knitter without Paradise.

After the Camp Fire (2018), knitters from around the world poured their kindness into our LYS, replacing knitting needles, spindles, yarn, bags, and accessories. With the smoke blocking the sun for a month, frigid temperatures arrived, and they sent us hats, sweaters, and scarves. They warmed our bodies and our souls.

Top Ten books?

Daniel Deronda by George Eliot • *Poor Folk* by Fyodor Dostoyevsky • *Bleak House* by Charles Dickens • *North and South* by Elizabeth Gaskell • *Persuasion* by Jane Austen • Poems of Emily Dickinson • *Let Go* by François Fénelon • *Knitters Almanac* by Elizabeth Zimmermann • Hebrew/English Tanakh • *Conscience and Courage* by Eva Fogelman

Project monogamy or cast on all the things?

I am giving my hand to monogamy post-fire, as so many things burned unfinished.

Favorite places to eat/drink/knit in SF?

The Samovar for tea, **Blue Bottle Coffee**, **Smittens**, **La Boulangerie de San Francisco**

Favorite places to eat/drink/knit in Paradise?

Coffee's On, **El Rancho**, **Sophia's Thai**, **Joylynn's Chocolates**, **Pile It High** frozen yogurt

Painted Lady

by Sonya Philip | 100 Acts of Sewing

In a city famous for its foggy weather, a cowl is a great way to keep out the chill. The stitch patterns on Painted Lady mimic the shiplap, shingles, and decorative elements of San Francisco's famous Victorians, all in a beautiful tricolor palette. The Painted Ladies of Alamo Square are distinguished by being painted three or more colors to enhance their Victorian era embellishments. You may recognize them from The Invasion of the Body Snatchers, The Five Year Engagement, Full House/Fuller House, or a postcard—they are a classic image of the city. Did you know that Alice Walker, author of The Color Purple, lived in one and used to host small Tracy Chapman concerts in her home? The Conversation and Mrs. Doubtfire were set and filmed nearby, too. Be sure to visit Alamo Square and see the Painted Ladies for yourself.

Twirl's Ditto enhances the coziness quotient of this cowl by combining multiple wools, alpaca, and mohair—those fibers bring an airy warmth to this cowl, and the color options are gorgeous.

Size
One Size

Materials
Twirl Yarn Ditto (a blend of Wensleydale, CVM, Alpaca, Kid Mohair; Sport weight: 125 yd/114 m per 1.76 oz/50 g skein)
  MC: Tide Pool, 1 skein
  CC1: Lichen, 1 skein
  CC2: Ether, 1 skein

US 6/4.0 mm 16-inch/40-cm circular needle

Stitch marker, tapestry needle

Gauge
21 sts x 30 rnds = 4 inches/10 cm in Stockinette stitch, after blocking

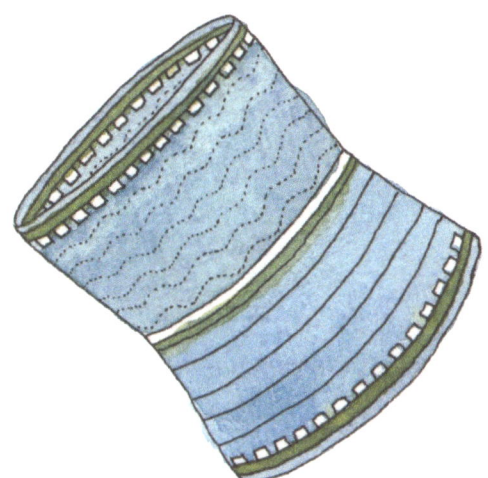

Finished Measurements
Height: 10 inches/25 cm
Circumference: 22 inches/56 cm

Twirl Yarn

With sheep, goats, alpacas, and a number of non-fiber creatures roaming the ranch, Twirl Yarn creates naturally-dyed yarns with fibers raised and plants grown on the ranch, including indigo, plus low-impact acid dyes. The yarns are a blend of fibers in a palette inspired by the beauty you can see on the ranch.

Twirl Yarn
Napa, CA
twirlyarn.com
@twirlyarn

Pattern

With MC yarn, using Long-Tail Cast-On, CO 108 sts. Join for working in the rnd, being careful not to twist, and pl m to indicate BOR.

Rnds 1, 3 & 5: Purl all sts.

Rnd 2: Knit all sts.

Rnd 4: Do not break yarn, change to CC1, knit all sts and carry MC up the back.

Rnd 6: Break CC1, change to CC2, knit all sts.

Corrugated Rib

Rnd 7: To work Corrugated Rib *bring CC2 to front, p2, move yarn to back, pick up MC, k2; rep from * to end of rnd. Carry yarn loosely in back when not in use.

Rnds 8–9: Work remainder of Corrugated Rib as est.

Shiplap

Rnd 10: Break CC2, change to MC, knit all sts.

Rnd 11: Purl all sts.

Rnds 12–36: Work Shiplap Rnds 1–5 five times.

Rnds 37–39: Knit all sts.

Color Band

Rnd 40: Break MC yarn, change to CC1, knit all sts.

Rnd 41, 43 & 45: Purl all sts.

Rnd 42: Break CC1, change to CC2, knit all sts.

Rnd 44: Knit all sts.

Shingles

Rnds 46–68: Work Shingles Rnds 1–6 four times.

Rnd 69: Knit all sts.

Corrugated Rib

Rnd 70 (Set up Corrugated Rib pattern): *With CC2, k2, with MC, k2; rep from * to end of rnd.

Rnds 71–73: Work Corrugated Rib.

Rnd 74: Do not break yarn, with CC2, knit all sts. Carry MC up the back.

Rnd 75: Break CC2, change to CC1, knit all sts.

Rnd 76, 78 & 80: Purl all sts with color used in previous rnd.

Rnd 77: Break CC1, change to MC, knit all sts.

Rnd 79: Knit all sts.

BO all sts loosely.

Finishing

Weave in all ends. Soak in lukewarm water with wool wash for ten minutes. Rinse and squeeze out water. Lay flat to dry, patting smooth to finished measurements.

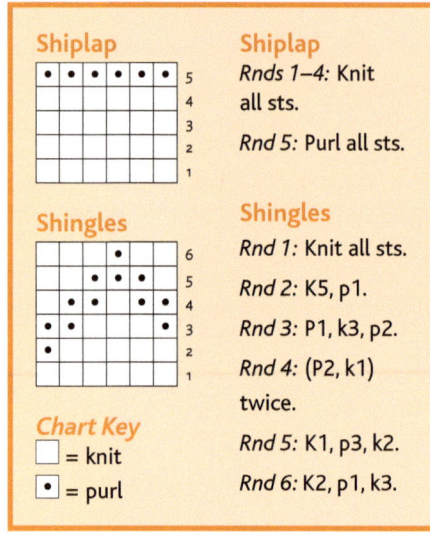

Shiplap

Shingles

Chart Key
- ☐ = knit
- ⊡ = purl

Shiplap

Rnds 1–4: Knit all sts.

Rnd 5: Purl all sts.

Shingles

Rnd 1: Knit all sts.

Rnd 2: K5, p1.

Rnd 3: P1, k3, p2.

Rnd 4: (P2, k1) twice.

Rnd 5: K1, p3, k2.

Rnd 6: K2, p1, k3.

Sonya loves San Francisco

What has your knitwear design journey been like?

Once I learned in the early 2000s, I knit at a fever pitch. Everybody received hats for presents. My skills grew, fed in large part by the way knitting merged with my growing digital life through photo sharing sites like Flickr and craft blogs. I imagined my pattern designs gracing the pages of *Knitty*. That hasn't yet happened, maybe one day! I have several knit toys I made for the pattern company KnitWhits and am slowly adding some accessories to my design tool kit. I would like to add a basic sweater to the mix, now I only need to find time to get that done.

Tell us about a hidden San Francisco treasure...

Sutro Baths at Lands End in the Outer Richmond. They are the remains of a large saltwater swimming pool and it's a beautiful place, with trails down to the water and along the coast.

Top Ten TV shows

1. *Broadchurch* 2. *Lewis* 3. *Miss Fisher's Murder Mystery* 4. *Endeavor* 5. *Vera* 6. *Poirot* 7. *Rosemary & Thyme* 8. *Forbrydelsen* (The Killing) 9. *Prime Suspect* 10. *Wallander*

Project monogamy or cast on all the things? Picker or thrower? MUNI knitting: must-have or never ever? Favorite line? Favorite neighborhood?

Definitely cast on ALL the things. I'm a bit of a magpie when it comes to making, my head always turned by the excitement of starting a shiny new project. I learned to knit English but taught myself how to throw, so now I do a weird hybrid of both. I hardly ever bring my knitting with me and when I do, I usually forget I have it. My favorite MUNI line is the F line, which uses vintage street cars from around the world. It runs down **Market Street** and along the **Embarcadero**. As for favorite neighborhood, I have to say my own neighborhood, the **Castro**.

Favorite places to knit in San Francisco?

My favorite place to knit is **Flora Grubb Gardens** in Bayview. There's a tiny coffee shop and places to sit, surrounded by gorgeous plants. On Saturdays there's a Farmers Market down the street. The nursery is the owner's actual name and whenever I visit, I dream of ways I could just move myself in.

Yerba Buena

by Juliana Lustenader

The Yerba Buena Poncho was inspired by Yerba Buena Gardens, a tranquil sanctuary nestled between the daunting high-rises of San Francisco's financial district. The gardens feature a sprawling lawn for visitors to lie upon while listening to the splashes of a wide, rushing waterfall which frames the city's Martin Luther King, Jr. Memorial. Tall arches shelter a rounded platform used as a stage for local musicians and performers during the summer months.

The lace pattern featured along the bottom edge of the Yerba Buena poncho echoes the rounded shapes found throughout the design of the gardens. The peaks of these rounded shapes are also reminiscent of the nearby Bay Bridge. The color and structure of the garment were inspired by the tall buildings framing the gardens' edges. Worked in Gather, a beautiful wool and alpaca blend, the Yerba Buena Poncho makes a lovely, drapey top layer for any San Francisco explorer.

The poncho is knit in two flat rectangular pieces from the bottom up, then seamed after blocking. Only a few inches over the shoulders and at each end of the rectangular pieces are seamed, leaving an open section over each arm. Though knit flat, it is recommended to use a long circular needle to accommodate all the stitches. The pattern comes with written and charted instructions for the lace motif. Below the lace pattern is a simple elongated stitch created over two rows using double yarnovers that are later dropped. It's a simple technique used to create a unique texture.

Size

Adult XS/S (M/L, 1X/2X)
Shown in size XS/S

Materials

A Verb for Keeping Warm Gather (75% Rambouillet, 25% Alpaca; Sport weight: 200 yd/182.8 m per 1.76 oz/50 g skein); color: Quartz; 5 (6, 8) skeins

US 7/4.5 mm 32-inch/80-cm circular needle

Stitch markers, tapestry needle, waste yarn

Gauge

20 sts x 32 rows = 4 inches/10 cm in Stockinette stitch, after blocking

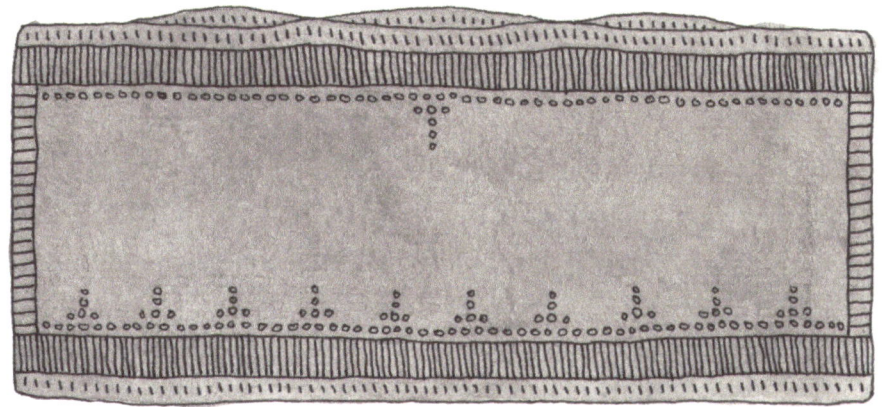

Finished Measurements

Wingspan/Length (longest side): 34 (37.5, 40.5) inches/86 (95, 103) cm
Depth/Width: 18 (21, 24) inches/46 (53, 61) cm from CO edge to shoulder

A Verb for Keeping Warm

Yarns from AVFKW are elegant, natural, and intensely personal. Because flocks and fiber mills change over time, new yarns are created (and old ones put to rest), but all are naturally-dyed or simply natural. AVFKW's yarns are full of passion and expertise.

A Verb for Keeping Warm
Oakland, CA
averbforkeepingwarm.com
@avfkw

Pattern

Back

CO 171 (187, 203) sts.

Row 1 (WS): Sl1, knit to end of row.

Row 2 (RS): Sl1, knit to end of row.

Row 3: Sl1, k3, pl m, purl to last 4 sts, pl m, k4.

Row 4: Sl1, knit to m, k1, (yo, k2tog) to m, knit to end of row.

Row 5: Sl1, knit to m, purl to m, knit to end of row.

Rows 6–8: Sl1, knit to end of row.

Row 9: P1, (yo twice, p1) to end of row.

Row 10: K1, (drop yos, k1) to end of row.

Rows 11–13: Sl1, purl to end of row.

Row 14: Sl1, purl to m, work Yerba Buena chart starting with Row 1 to m, purl to end of row.

Rep Row 14 working chart between markers for the next 12 rows.

Row 15: Sl1, purl to end of row.

Row 16: Sl1, purl to m, knit to m, purl to end of row.

Rep Rows 15–16 until piece measures 15 ½ (18 ½, 21 ½) inches/40.5 (48, 56) cm. Rep Row 15 once more.

Row 17: Sl1, purl to m, k1, (yo, k2tog) to m, purl to end of row.

Rows 18–20: Sl1, purl to end of row.

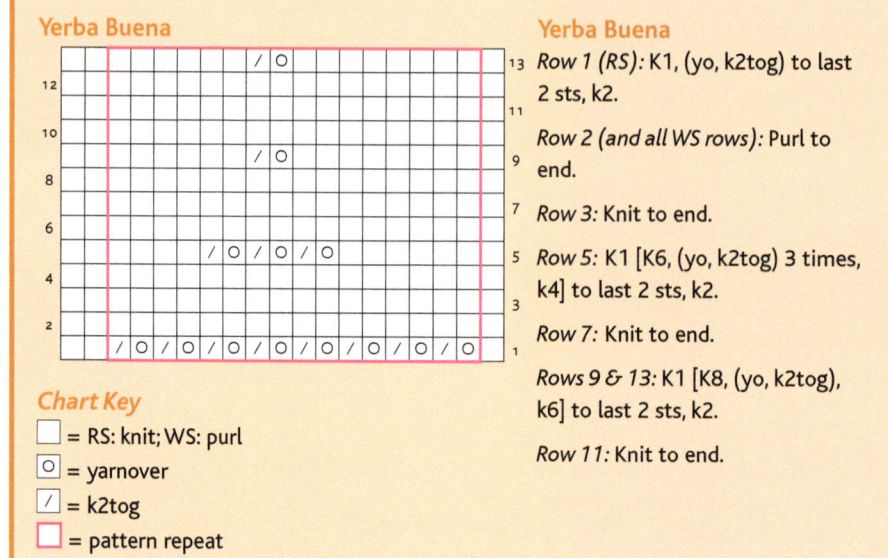

Yerba Buena

Chart Key

☐ = RS: knit; WS: purl
◯ = yarnover
╱ = k2tog
▭ = pattern repeat

Yerba Buena

Row 1 (RS): K1, (yo, k2tog) to last 2 sts, k2.

Row 2 (and all WS rows): Purl to end.

Row 3: Knit to end.

Row 5: K1 [K6, (yo, k2tog) 3 times, k4] to last 2 sts, k2.

Row 7: Knit to end.

Rows 9 & 13: K1 [K8, (yo, k2tog), k6] to last 2 sts, k2.

Row 11: Knit to end.

Row 21: K1, (yo twice, k1) to end of row.

Row 22: P1, (drop yos, p1) to end of row.

Rows 23–25: Sl1, knit to end of row.

Row 26: Sl1, knit to m, purl to m, knit to end of row.

Row 27: Sl1, knit to m, k1, (yo, k2tog) to m, knit to end of row.

Row 28: Sl1, knit to m, purl to m, knit to end of row.

Rows 29–30: Sl1, knit to end of row.

BO all sts.

Front

Work same as Back to Row 16. Rep Rows 15–16 until piece measures 14 (17, 20) inches/35.5 (43, 51) cm. Rep Row 15 once more.

Row 1 (RS): Sl1, purl to m, k81 (89, 97), yo, k2tog, knit to m, purl to end of row.

Rows 2, 4, 6, 8, 10 & 12 (WS): Sl1, purl to end of row.

Rows 3, 7 & 11: Sl1, purl to m, knit to m, purl to end of row.

Row 5: Sl1, purl to m, k81 (89, 97), yo, k2tog, knit to m, purl to end of row.

Row 9: Sl1, purl to m, k79 (87, 95), [yo, k2tog] 3 times, knit to m, purl to end of row.

Work Rows 17–30 of Back instructions.

BO all sts.

Finishing

Weave in all ends. Soak pieces in lukewarm water with wool wash for ten minutes. Rinse and squeeze out water. Lay flat to dry, patting smooth to finished measurements.

Hold pieces with WS facing each other and BO edges held together.

Left Edge: Starting at left edge, seam BO edges of front and back together for 5 (5 ½, 6) inches/13 (14, 15) cm. Cut yarn.

Top Left Shoulder: Measure 12 (13, 14) inches/30.5 (33, 35.5) cm from left edge and seam ½ inch/1 cm. Cut yarn.

Seam the Right Edge and Top Right Shoulder the same as Left Edge and Top Left Shoulder.

Weave in remaining ends

Jules loves San Francisco

What has your knitwear design journey been like?

The summer after I graduated from college, I got a job at **ImagiKnit**, the largest yarn store in San Francisco. I was inspired daily by the yarn surrounding me and knew pretty quickly that I wanted to design my own accessories and garments. I shared my ideas with a coworker and she helped me write and test knit my first pattern, a colorwork hat, in 2014. I was shocked by how many knitters made and loved the pattern on Ravelry. Since then, I've learned many more skills and have dived into designing garments and larger items. Many of my designs are inspired by the streets and neighborhoods of San Francisco, the best city in the world! Though I no longer work at Imagiknit, I still shop there often and use their yarns in my designs.

Tell us a San Francisco story...

Once, I was knitting in **Dolores Park** and saw Jonathan Groff walking down the street. He was heading to the park to film an episode of *Looking*, a show that takes place in San Francisco. I ran up to him and told him how I'm an actor who recently performed in a local production of *Spring Awakening*, the Broadway show that gave him so much fame. He then insisted on taking a photo together that reenacted the Broadway poster. It's one of my favorite pictures and memories.

Top Ten (movies, songs, books, TV shows)

Too hard to answer, sorry!

MUNI knitting: must-have or never ever? Favorite station? Favorite neighborhood?

I always bring smaller knitting projects with me on MUNI so I have something to do in the tunnels during my commute. My favorite station in the city would have to be **Castro Station**, mainly because I love the neighborhood. But my favorite neighborhood would have to be the **Outer Sunset**, by the beach where I live. Nothing beats searching for sand dollars and seaglass on **Ocean Beach** on a beautiful day.

Picker or thrower? Project monogamy or cast on all the things?

Thrower! I also cast on all the things. How can anyone stick to one project at a time? There are so many lovely patterns out there!

Favorite places to eat, drink, and knit in SF?

For brunch, I love eating at **Outerlands** restaurant on Judah Street. Their menu changes often, but is always delicious. After your meal, you can take a nice walk along **Ocean Beach** or in **Golden Gate Park**, which are both close by.

If you're looking for music with your drinks, I highly recommend visiting **Martuni's**, a piano bar nearby on Market and Valencia. Their martinis are dangerously tasty, and you're likely to hear major talent at the mic and keys, sometimes Broadway stars who stop by on their days off from their Bay Area tours.

San Francisco boasts a plethora of parks. I love sitting and knitting in the grass of **Dolores Park** in the Mission, **Yerba Buena Park** downtown, and the sprawling lawns in **Golden Gate Park**.

18th & Castro

by Kathleen Dames & Vilasinee Bunnag | Loome

"And you gotta give 'em hope. Hope for a better world, hope for a better tomorrow, hope for a better place to come to if the pressures at home are too great. Hope that all will be all right."
—Harvey Milk

With Garter stitch edges and a Stockinette body, this slouchy top with lowered armholes knits up in no time with simple construction that is perfect for layering. The party gets going with an exuberance* of pom poms placed as you wish: along the neckline, scattered all over as shown, spelling out LOVE—the possibilities are endless! For the pom poms I turned to the expert, Loome founder Vilasinee Bunnag, who showed me some of the many pom pom options you can create with a Loome tool (plus tassels, braids, and more), and we created a rainbow of pom poms to adorn this top.

When you're strolling the rainbow crosswalk at the intersection of Castro and 18th, or wherever you are, show off your pride and exuberance with this top.

*If that's not the name for a group of pom poms, it should be.

Notes
- Top is worked from the bottom up, beginning in the round, then front and back are split and worked back-and-forth for the armholes, before being rejoined to work the yoke in the round with a series of decreases to shape the shoulders.
- Pom poms are optional. Work them in any yarn you have. They are great stashbusters. As shown we created two pom poms in each color of Little Skein's Rainbow mini-set, with yarn leftover for more. We chose to create starburst pom poms and only attached them to the front of the garment (leaning back on pom poms seemed potentially uncomfortable), but pom pom density and placement are knitter's choice.

Sizes
Adult XS (S, M, L, 1X, 2X, 3X, 4X, 5X, 6X)
Shown in size S with 2 ¼ inches/5.5 cm positive ease

Materials
Top: Little Skein in the Big Wool House Sock (90% Targhee Wool, 10% Nylon; Fingering weight: 410 yd/375 m per 3.53 oz/100 g); color: Gotta Give 'Em Hope (Harvey Milk); 2 (2, 3, 3, 3, 4, 4, 4, 5, 5) skeins or approx. 650 (725, 875, 1000, 1150, 1275, 1400, 1550, 1700, 1875) yds

Pom poms: **Little Skein in the Big Wool House Sock & House Twist** (90% Targhee Wool, 10% Nylon; Fingering weight: 410 yd/375 m per 3.53 oz/100 g); color: Little Skein's Rainbow; seven 100 yd/91 m per 0.88 oz/25 g mini skeins

US 4/3.5 mm 29-inch/73-cm circular needle

Stitch markers; removable stitch markers; tapestry needle; scissors; Loome 5-in-1 Tool; Loome Pom Pom Trim Guide or 1.75-inch/4.5 cm cardboard round; DMC Embroidery Floss (preferably similar colors to your pom pom yarns): 8 inches/20 cm per pom pom

Gauge
24 sts x 32 rows/rnds = 4 inches/10 cm in Stockinette stitch, after blocking

Little Skein in the Big Wool

Do you like books, yarn, and project bags from a values-led business? Little Skein in the Big Wool centers love of literature and knitting while focusing on progressive values. The online shop is filled with charming kits, hand-dyed yarn (in-house and in partnership with special guest dyers), illustrated project bags of all shapes and sizes, and more.

Little Skein in the Big Wool
San Francisco, CA
littleskein.com
@littleskeinanne

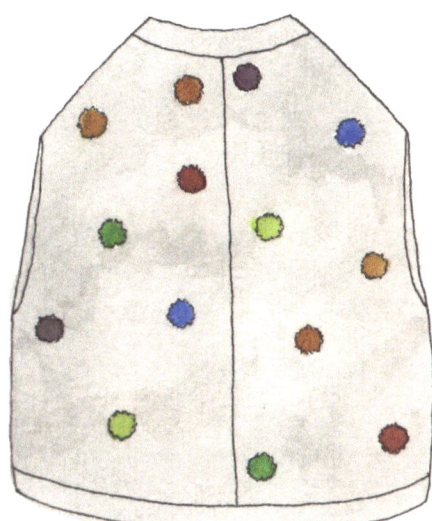

Finished Measurements
Hip Circumference: 28 (32, 36, 40, 44, 48, 52, 56, 60, 64) inches/71 (81, 91.5, 101.5, 112, 122, 132, 142, 152.5, 162.5) cm
Bust Circumference: 32 ¼ (36 ¼, 40 ¼, 44 ¼, 48 ¼, 52 ¼, 56 ¼, 60 ¼, 64 ¼, 68 ¼) inches/82 (92, 102, 112, 122.5, 132.5, 143, 153, 163) cm
Length to Underarm: 7 inches/17.75 cm for all sizes
Armhole Depth: 6 (6.5, 7, 7.5, 8, 8.5, 9, 9.5, 10, 10.5) inches/15 (16.5, 17.5, 19, 20.5, 21.5, 23, 24, 25.5, 26.5) cm
Yoke Depth: 6 ¼ (6 ½, 6 ¾, 7, 7 ¼, 7 ½, 7 ¾, 8, 8 ¼, 8 ½) inches/16 (16.5, 17, 17.5, 18.5, 19, 19.5, 20.5, 21, 21.5) cm
Overall Length: 21¼ (22, 22 ¾, 23 ½, 24 ¼, 25, 25 ¾, 26 ½, 27 ¼, 28) inches/54 (56, 57.75, 59.5, 61.5, 63.5, 65.5, 67, 69, 71) cm

Pattern

Body
With Top yarn CO 170 (194, 218, 242, 266, 290, 314, 338, 362, 386) sts. Work back-and-forth in Garter Stitch for 12 rows. Join for working in the rnd, pl BOR m.

Set-up Rnd: *K42 (48, 54, 60, 66, 72, 78, 84, 90, 96) sts, sl1 p-wise wyib and pl removable m in slipped st, k42 (48, 54, 60, 66, 72, 78, 84, 90, 96) sts, pl m; rep from * once more. Sl marked sts p-wise wyib every other rnd and move marker up as needed.

Inc Rnd: *K1, m1-L, work in est patts to 1 st before side m, m1-R, k1, sl m; rep from * once more to BOR m—4 sts inc'd.

Work seven rnds even, slipping marked sts every other rnd.

Rep these eight rnds six times total—194 (218, 242, 266, 290, 314, 338, 362, 386, 410) sts.

Split Body
Work back and forth as follows.

Split Row (RS): Work across 97 (109, 121, 133, 145, 157, 169, 181, 193, 205) sts to side m, turn.

WS Row: Sl1, k2, p91 (103, 115, 127, 139, 151, 163, 175, 187, 199) sts, k3.

RS Row: Sl1, work in est patts to end of row.

Rep these two rows until flat section measures 6 (6 ½, 7, 7 ½, 8, 8 ½, 9, 9 ½, 10, 10 ½) inches/15.25 (16.5, 17.75, 19, 20.25, 21.5, 22.75, 24, 25.5, 26.5) cm, break yarn. With RS facing, slip just-worked sts along ndl to end of row. Rejoin yarn to begin working back sts. Work back as for front from Split Body. Do not break yarn.

Yoke
Rejoin sts for working in the rnd and work one rnd, slipping marked sts every other rnd to maintain patt.

Work 10 (0, 4, 0, 0, 0, 0, 0, 4, 0) rnds in est patts.

Yoke Dec Rnd: Sl1 k-wise wyib, *knit to 1 st before m'ed st, s2kpo, knit to 1 st before m, sl st to right ndl, remove m, return st to left ndl, pl m, s2kpo; rep from * once more using st slipped at beg of rnd for last dec—8 sts dec'd.

Work 3 (3, 3, 3, 3, 3, 3, 1, 1) rnds even in est patts.

Rep these 4 (4, 4, 4, 4, 4, 4, 2, 2) rnds 10 (13, 10, 10, 9, 7, 6, 4, 31, 34) times total—114 (114, 162, 186, 218, 258, 300, 330, 138, 138) sts.

For sizes M (L, 1X, 2X, 3X, 4X) only:
Work Yoke Dec Rnd, then work 1 rnd even in est patts 5 (8, 11, 16, 19, 24) times—122 (122, 130, 130, 138, 138) sts.

For all sizes:
Work in the rnd in Garter Stitch for 12 rnds. BO all sts loosely p-wise.

Finishing
Seam hem together. Weave in all ends. Soak in lukewarm water with wool wash for ten minutes. Rinse and squeeze out water. Lay flat to dry, patting smooth to finished measurements.

With Pom pom yarn and Loome tool make 0.75-inch/2-cm diameter pom poms (see sidebar). As shown you will need two pom poms of each color.

Attach pom poms to your sweater by threading each side of the yarn or floss onto the inside of your sweater. To make the pom pom removable, simply tie a bow tie. To make the pom poms permanent, tie double knots and weave the ends into the garment, then trim the ends.

Making Pom Poms

This video from Loome will help you make a starburst pom pom: *https://www.youtube.com/watch?v=7qZ8GJ_7e-o*
Or visit *theloome.com* to learn more.

1. Secure the end of your yarn to any of the notches on the Loome tool and wind 75 revolutions. Don't wind too tight or too loose.
2. When finished, secure the end of the yarn to any of the notches again and cut, leaving a 1-inch/2.5-cm tail.
3. Cut an 8-inch/20-cm piece of embroidery floss and split the floss into three plies. You'll now have two 8-inch pieces.
4. Take one of the three-plied embroidery floss pieces and thread it under the yarn bundle. Make a single tie so it lands in the middle of the yarn bundle. Do not close the knot.
5. Flip the tool so the backside is facing up and make a surgeon's knot or two overhand knots, making sure the floss is centered. Now pull so that the knot is snug but not tight, then pull the entire yarn bundle off the tool.
6. Working close to the knot, pull hard so that the knot is tight and quickly close with two more ties. Cut the tails leaving ¼-inch/0.6-cm.
7. Cut through the loops on both sides of the bundle.
8. With the pom pom trim guide, hold it over the center of the pom pom and trim the pom pom to the shape of the trim guide. Once done, flip the pom pom over with one turn and rep the step so that the pom pom is trimmed all around.
9. Cut an 8-inch/20-cm piece of yarn or floss to tie the pom pom to your top. Thread it with a needle, then run it under the tight middle floss of the pom pom. Remove the needle and tie a tight double knot so the yarn or floss is secured to the middle floss.

Vilasinee loves San Francisco

What are your favorite places to eat in San Francisco?

- Great Fast Meal: **Souvla**—Always reliable tasty Greek food, and they have Greek yogurt in those old school blue and white coffee cups that makes me nostalgic for NYC.
- Hawaii Food Done Right: **Liho Liho**. By far my favorite place in SF that's worth lining up for at 4:30 pm. So fun and delicious. One time we were told by the waiter that he thought we ordered too much food … that's how we roll!
- Friday Night Trucks: **Off the Grid @ Fort Mason**—A fun San Francisco experience with views of the **Golden Gate Bridge**.
- Awesome Sit Down: **Al's Place**—Mostly vegetarian (with some seafood thrown in) fine dining in the **Mission**. I love this place.
- Farmers Markets Eats: **Ferry Building** on Saturdays. Farmers markets are such a great way to experience the abundance of California produce and good eats. This one is so good.
- Best Restaurant Visits and Reviews: **The Infatuation**—their restaurant visit Instagram Stories are so good.

The 3-Day Yarn Crawl*

by Kathleen Dames & Alice O'Reilly

*Professional stunt knitters. Do not try this at home.

Sweet ride (not ours)

Be sure to ask the staff at each shop for their recommendations. We discovered tasty local cafés (and the best things to try) that we might not have found out about otherwise. While we have shared a few of those places in the LYS profiles on the following pages, new spots are opening all the time.

Day One: San Francisco

On our first day, we visited the LYSes in the city: **Atelier Yarns** in the Lower Pacific Heights, **Firebird Yarns** in Haight-Ashbury, and **ImagiKnit** in the Castro, plus justly-famous **Britex Fabrics** in the Financial District. Both 30-year-old Atelier Yarns and ImagiKnit (at 17 years) are long-standing, full-service shops deeply rooted in their communities; year-old Firebird Yarns has built a strong local following and should have a bright future alongside the other two SF LYSes. If you are a local, of course you will have your favorite; if you are visiting, each shop will take you to a different quintessential SF neighborhood, so you will have the opportunity to get to know various parts of the city.

Love Fest Fibers at ImagiKnit

California car culture is most definitely a thing, which is why we decided to rent some wheels and spread our LYS recommendations over so many square miles—from our northern to southern-most LYS, it's about 175 miles. Our itinerary begins in the city, on foot, in cabs, and riding cable cars. For two people used to walking everywhere, the visceral realization that walking from here to there in San Francisco is a physical challenge, thanks to those famous hills, led to a deeper understanding of just how public transport works in SF, as well as to a meeting of the minds with a cab driver (as convenient as hailing a ride with your phone may be, our cab driver knew where he was taking us without consulting a screen).

On our second and third days, we got behind the wheel and headed out to the ocean, the redwoods, and the vineyards of the greater Bay Area. Of course, you may visit any (or all) of the yarn shops however you like. To be honest, unless you are professional fiber explorers like us (ha!), we recommend taking it a little slower and enjoying more of what each part of the greater Bay Area has to offer before plunging on to the next LYS. One of the things we really loved about many of the area LYSes is their relationships with local fiber folks and their focus on inclusivity in their local fiber community.

Lombard St—SF streets are no joke!

Britex's location in the Financial District is, perhaps, the least exciting from the outside, but once you enter this fabric paradise, you may not want to leave—don't forget all the trims and notions up on the second floor.

Let us reiterate here that what may look like an easy walk from one part of the city to another may end up leaving you exhausted and blistered. Definitely make use of public transportation, cabs, ride-hailing services, or your own car.

Day Two: Sonoma & Napa Counties and East Bay

Sunny corner at Cast Away

Drive north across the **Golden Gate Bridge** and, if you don't detour to **Atelier Marin** (sister shop of Atelier Yarns), **Muir Woods**, or **Point Reyes**, you can visit **Cast Away Yarn Shop** in about an hour. You could make a weekend of it in Santa Rosa, which boasts charming shops, the **Charles M. Schulz Museum**, and historic stone lodging **Hotel la Rose**. If you have a fiber-based interest, Cast Away has supplies for you.

After coffee and yarn in Railroad Square (Santa Rosa's historic district), we pointed the car to Napa County seat, Napa, and rolled through the county's famous vineyards to our next stop, **Yarns On First**. This little shop on the town's main shopping street has a community table in the front, and the staff shared a wealth of local knowledge with us, when we asked for some late lunch recommendations, including a visit to **Napa Bookmine** at the **Oxbow Public Market**. Rain meant we couldn't sit outside at the market, but that just meant we got to look around at all the stands inside while we were waiting for our lunch—a good problem to have in an area known for fresh produce, innovative food, and outstanding wine (make sure you have a designated driver if you are going to partake).

Indigo bunches drying at AVFKW

Next stop was the Berkeley area (Albany, Berkeley, and Oakland), home to three excellent LYSes: **Avenue Yarns**, **The Black Squirrel**, and **A Verb for Keeping Warm**. You might consider visiting them by crossing the Bay from San Francisco by BART, ferry, or Bay Bridge, rather than following our route. All three shops offer beautiful yarns in their own unique, welcoming spaces. We saw a busy classroom at Avenue Yarns, the end of a leather sandal-making class at The Black Squirrel, and got a tour of the dye garden and studio at AVFKW. We finished our day by dining with two of the Bay Area's most innovative fiber folks, Vilasinee Bunnag, founder of **The Loome**, and Julie Weisenberger, founder of **Cocoknits**. You will find their elegant supplies and books in stores throughout the Bay Area (and the world)—anything from either brand will make an excellent addition to your fiber supply kit.

Old school dining at Nick's

Day Three: Peninsula, Monterey Bay & Santa Cruz

After brunch with many of our contributors (designers and dyers) organized by Trish Richman, at **Nick's Rockaway** and wiping the salt spray off our windshield, we descended *en masse* upon **The Royal Bee Yarn Company**. They made us all feel welcome in their cozy space steps from the ocean. As in other parts of the world, we loved seeing a variety of people come together over knitting.

After hugs and yarn, we headed down to Monterey Bay to visit **Monarch Knitting**, named after the butterfly that calls Pacific Grove one of its migratory homes. We first met the Monarch crew at Stitches West, and they were just as friendly on their home turf. As a bonus we got to meet up with Sarah Pedersen, owner of The Dye Project, who recently relocated to the area, then we caravanned with Sarah up to **Yarn Shop Santa Cruz** to finish our adventure in fiber travel in a modern, cozy space with strong support for the local artistic community.

Salty air on the Peninsula

San Francisco

Atelier Yarns
1945 Divisadero St, Pacific Heights, San Francisco
Tel: (415) 771-1550
Website: atelieryarns.com • Instagram: @atelieryarns

A sharp black & white awning above a white brick storefront serves as the perfect foil to the well-organized riot of color inside Atelier Yarns. Work your way around Amanda Madlener's floor-to-ceiling shelves to check out all their offerings, from workhorse to cashmere to fun fur (on hand for chemo caps and ... fun), all arranged by weight. The shop has an extensive list of classes in knitting, crochet, and weaving. We found the staff so helpful and friendly—they are excited to help you but are also happy to let you browse on your own. They even sent us around the corner right before closing to sample the *Koign Amann* at **b. patisserie**. We highly recommend following their advice and fueling up with some coffee and treats before or after stocking up on all the yarn, notions, and books you might need.

There is also a second location, **Atelier Marin**, in San Anselmo. So, if you're heading north to Marin, be sure to stop by.

Photo credit: Atelier Yarns

Firebird Yarns
1322 Haight St, Haight-Ashbury, San Francisco
Tel: (415) 795-1229
Website: firebirdyarns.com • Instagram: @firebirdyarns

San Francisco's newest LYS, in a space with big plate glass windows and vintage charm, is colorful and friendly with plenty of indie-dyed yarns from local and regional dyers. No fears of a yarn desert here! Kathryn Bernard's space is open and airy with yarn skeins hung on the walls, making it easy to see them all, and a cozy couch for social knitting in the back. Check out hand-dyed yarns from Seismic Yarns, Comma Chameleon, Buxom Cat, and more. They also have a good selection of classic yarns to balance out the enthusiastic color. Follow Firebird's Instagram feed for upcoming area events, unboxing videos, and more. Everyone on staff are friendly and helpful.

Need another coffee? **Ritual Coffee Roasters** are on the corner with lots of carefully brewed coffees, beans roasted on site, and terrarium workshops to chill out after all that excellent coffee.

Photo credit: Firebird Yarns

San Francisco

ImagiKnit
3897 18th St, The Castro, San Francisco • Tel: (415) 621-6642
Website: imagiknit.com • Instagram: @theimagiknit
Situated on the first floor of a converted Victorian, ImagiKnit's entrance is under the building's turret on the corner. When you enter Allison Isaac's shop, you will find yourself in a large, colorful, fiber-filled room with a second room through an archway with more fiber-y treats and enticing samples. The large selection of yarns is organized by weight, and the staff will help you find whatever you are looking for. ImagiKnit also stocks a large array of notions and accessories, plus books and kits. There are couches and chairs to sit and knit or just ponder your next project. ImagiKnit also has an e-commerce site.

Need a treat? **Le Marais Bakery** (one of three in the city) is cater-corner from the shop with a tasty combo of French and Californian food and drink, from Avocado Toast to Pain Au Chocolat washed down with coffee, tea, or a cocktail in a lovely, light-filled space with pretty tiles. We met up with Brit-Marie to talk about Love Fest Fibers before heading across the street to see her jumbo balls of yarn in person.
Photo credit: ImagiKnit

Britex
117 Post St, Financial District, San Francisco • Tel: (415) 392-2910
Website: britexfabrics • Instagram: @britexfabrics
While we are first and foremost yarn people, we never say "no" to a fabric or button store, and, goodness, does Britex deliver. This San Francisco landmark recently moved to new digs, with most fabric on the street level in an airy double-height space (ask for help getting that bolt of fabric from the top shelf). From silks to Missoni knits plus a rainbow of solids, you can find all sorts of treasures here. Upstairs you will find a wall of buttons (not self-service, which is a little different from what we are used to), aisles of notions, tools, trims, and findings, plus more fabric, including indigo-dyed imports from Japan (we may be a little obsessed). Locals miss the original location, but who amongst us loves change? We found the staff helpful and friendly but not pushy. This is not a bargain place (they even have Chanel tweed fabric for when you're ready to make your own Chanel jacket), but if you are looking for something special and/or particular (or even just looking), this is a can't-miss spot.
Photo credit: Kathleen Dames & Alice O'Reilly

Sonoma & Napa Counties

Cast Away Yarn Shop

100 Fourth Street, Santa Rosa • Tel: (707) 546-9276
Website: castawayyarnshop.com • Instagram: @castawayyarnshop

Owned by mother-daughter duo, Justine and Cleo Malone, with their Boston Terrier Olive by their side, Cast Away Yarn Shop in Sonoma County is one of the largest craft stores in Northern California. With supplies and tools for knitting, crochet, felting, needle punch, weaving, and more, this open and airy shop in a historic warehouse building may well have everything you need. And some of it is stocked in a "cast away" sailboat that they reclaimed with a crocheted sail. In addition to stocking yarns from companies like Berocco and Malabrigo, they also carry regional favorites like The Dye Project and Twirl, as well as far away ones like Hedgehog Fibres and June Cashmere. Beyond their extensive array of supplies and their wall of knitted samples, Cast Away has their own interactive online knitting and crochet pattern reading program, Placemaker, which Cleo developed while in college.

  Note: The address is on Fourth Street, but the entrance to the shop is around the corner on Wilson.

Photo credit: Cast Away Yarn Shop

Yarns On First

1305 1st St, Napa • Tel: (707) 257-1363
Website: yarnsonfirst.com • Instagram: @yarnsonfirst

One county over is another mother-daughter yarn shop with a cozy space organized by color. Don't panic if you need a particular weight! Marcie, Jess, and their staff know where everything is and are happy to help you find just what you need. The chromatic scheme allows you to think about knitting and crochet in a different way, plus you feel like you're shopping in a rainbow. They stock an array of yarns from truly local companies, Sincere Sheep (Brooke Sinnes lives nearby and teaches classes here) and Twirl Yarn (Mary Pettis-Sarley's ranch is also in Napa). Yarns from Urth, BC Garn, and more make this a well-stocked shop that also offers a variety of classes and workshops. Don't miss their selection of buttons, bags, and books. A member of the Shop Local movement, they also give excellent recommendations for other shops and restaurants to visit in the area.

Photo credit: Yarns On First

East Bay

Avenue Yarns
1325 Solano Ave, Albany • Tel: (510) 526-9276
Website: avenueyarns.com • Instagram: @avenueyarns

Just north of Berkeley, friendly and colorful Avenue Yarns is the kind of local yarn store that makes you feel like a local right away. Filled with lovely yarns, helpful staff, and friendly knitters who are always happy to show off their latest project, they also offer Knit Labs, community events, and an ever-expanding array of classes. Owners Rebekah Porter and Karen King focus on their local customers, but visitors like us feel just as welcome. Don't miss their selection of knit-inspired ceramics, plus some of the prettiest turned-wood tools from local artisan David Earls: spindles, yarn bowls, and trinket boxes perfect for corralling all your stitch markers, all made from found wood.

Avenue Yarns is located right across the street from destination plant nursery, **Flowerland**, which also houses **Highwire Coffee** in a vintage airstream on their grounds. The shop is surrounded by great restaurants and cafes.

Photo credit: Avenue Yarns

The Black Squirrel
Flagship: 651 Addison St STE B, Berkeley • Tel: (510) 561-3680
Website: blacksquirrelberkeley.com
Instagram: @blacksquirrelberkeley
Annex: 470G 49th St, Oakland • Tel: (510) 561-3680
Website: blackquirreloakland.com
Instagram: @blacksquirreloakland

Even on a rainy day, The Black Squirrel is bright and colorful, from its wall of indie-dyed yarn to its tables of craft supplies. Chase Clark started The Black Squirrel in 2016 and expanded with an Annex in Temescal Alley a couple of months after our visit. Not only does the bright, modern space hold supplies for a variety of crafts, but it also has a large classroom space outfitted with sewing machines, weaving and spinning tools, and a lending library of vintage books. We got to see a leather sandal class in action, where everyone was having so much fun. Both spaces are welcoming, inclusive, sustainable, highly curated, and focus on stocking US-based women-owned brands. The annex is closer to public transportation, while the flagship hosts classes and has more elbow room. Next time we plan to visit both!

Photo credit: The Black Squirrel

East Bay

A Verb for Keeping Warm
6328 San Pablo Ave, Oakland • Tel: (510) 595-8372
Website: averbforkeepingwarm.com • Instagram: @avfkw
From the thought-provoking name to the rafters filled with drying indigo, and all the warm, bright, thoughtful spaces in between, A Verb for Keeping Warm (Verb or AVFKW for short) is a can't-miss destination for fiber and natural dye enthusiasts. Their inclusive, welcoming space houses an outstanding collection of house yarns, as well as an elegant selection from other companies, like Biches et Buches, Daughter of a Shepherd, Spincycle, and more. In addition to knitting and crochet supplies, you will find natural dye (co-owner Kristine Vejar is *The Natural Dyer*, after all, and co-owner Adrienne Rodriguez is an expert in mushroom dyeing), sewing, quilting, and spinning supplies from Liberty, Merchant & Mills, and others. When you have finished checking out all the beautiful samples, take a peek at the dye garden out back. An important part of the local community, AVFKW hosts community knitting, a variety of classes, and trunk shows with a friendly and helpful staff of ten women.
Photo credit: Elysa Weitala for A Verb for Keeping Warm

Peninsula

The Royal Bee Yarn Company
90 Eureka Dr, Pacifica • Tel: (650) 898-8329
Website: theroyalbeeyarncompany.com
Instagram: @theroyalbeeyarncompany
With honey-colored walls and a velvet couch, could Kelley Corten have called her shop anything but The Royal Bee Yarn Company? A colorful, welcoming place with a nice variety of yarns, including their own eco-friendly line, we felt right at home here. Beyond yarn, in their online shop and in-store, they have a great selection of fiber, notions, and their own line of well-designed project bags (think lots of different pockets!), created in collaboration with local fiber friend extraordinaire, Trish Richman, the friendly force behind Carpe Yarn. The Royal Bee's yarn is spun from 18-micron Merino wool into five weights from fingering to super bulky and dyed locally, then the colors are named after favorite customers. The Pacific Ocean is out the front door and across the road—you can walk to the beach. Who could ask for a better location? Classes, private events, and knit nights are all part of the friendly experience.
Photo credit: The Royal Bee Yarn Company

Monterey Bay & Santa Cruz

Monarch Knitting
529 Central Ave #4, Pacific Grove • Tel: (831) 647-9276
Website: monarchknitting.com • Instagram: @monarchknitting
Walk into this sun-filled space, and you will immediately feel both calm and excited. Monarch Knitting is roomy and colorful with yarn carefully organized throughout the store—so many possibilities in a serene space. You will find yarn from Shibui, The Fibre Company, The Farmers Daughter Fibers, and more. Also well-stocked with needles, notions, and bags, you could spend hours here enjoying the camaraderie of the big table by the windows or deciding what to cast on next. If you are looking to have someone else make the decision, they have a generous selection of kits, too. Ann Patterson and her staff (plus shop dog Linus) will help you find what you are looking for or let you follow your bliss. They have a calendar of classes and events, plus social knitting and crocheting regularly. Not far from the **Monterey Bay Aquarium** and **Cannery Row**, be sure to add this shop to your itinerary or visit them at Stitches West—they practically bring the whole shop with them!
Photo credit: Monarch Knitting

Yarn Shop Santa Cruz
765 Cedar St #103, Santa Cruz • Tel: (831) 515-7966
Website: yarnshopsantacruz.com • Instagram: @yarnshopsantacruz
Cozy, friendly, and colorful, this little shop a block from Santa Cruz's Front Street is staffed by owner Cory and her friendly, helpful team. They may be small, but they have a lovely selection of yarns including Jamieson & Smith, Mrs Crosby, and The Dye Project—they're Sarah's LYS. Locally made cards, project bags, and the *Hands Full* zine make you feel right at home, as does their nicely curated selection of books and magazines from Amirisu, Pom Pom Quarterly, Making, and others. In addition to a range of classes, don't miss their morning Tea & Stitching and evening Sweater Support, KAL, and Night Stitch gatherings, all listed on their website.
Photo credit: Sarah Pedersen

Abbreviations

approx = approximately

BO = bind off

BOR = beginning of round

cn = cable needle

CO = cast on

cont = continue

dec('d) = decrease(d)

est = established

inc('d) = increase(d)

k = knit

k-wise = knitwise

k1-tbl = knit stitch through the back loop to twist

k2tog = knit two together—1 stitch decreased

LH = left hand

m = marker

m1-L = make one stitch using backwards loop—1 stitch increased

m1-Lp = make one stitch using backwards loop purlwise—1 stitch increased

m1-R = make one stitch using backwards loop twisted in the opposite direction of m1-L—1 stitch increased

m1-Rp = make one stitch using backwards loop twisted in the opposite direction of m1-L purlwise—1 stitch increased

ndl = needle

p = purl

p-wise = purlwise

pl = place

p2tog = purl two together—1 stitch decreased

RH = right hand

RS = right side

sl = slip

ssk = slip first stitch knitwise, slip second stitch knitwise, knit two together—1 stitch decreased

s2kpo = slip two stitches together knitwise, knit one, pass two slipped stitches over—2 stitches decreased

st(s) = stitch(es)

-tbl = through the back loop(s)

WS = wrong side

wyib = with yarn in back (also wyb)

wyif = with yarn in front

w&t = wrap and turn = slip next stitch from left needle to right, bring working yarn from current position between needles to front/back, turn work, then slip stitch back from left needle to right and bring working yarn between needles to work next row, wrapping slipped stitch with a loop of yarn

yo = yarn over—1 stitch increased

1/1 LC = slip 1 to cable needle and hold to front, k1, k1 from cable needle

1/1 RC = slip 1 to cable needle and hold to back, k1, k1 from cable needle

2/2 KPRC = slip 2 to cable needle and hold to back, k2, p2 from cable needle

2/2 KPLC = slip 2 to cable needle and hold to front, p2, k2 from cable needle

2/2 LC = slip 2 to cable needle and hold to front, p2, k2 from cable needle

2/2 RC = slip 2 to cable needle and hold to back, k2, k2 from cable needle

Stitches

Garter Stitch (worked flat)
All Rows: Knit all sts.

Garter Stitch (worked in the rnd)
Rnd 1: Knit all sts.
Rnd 2: Purl all sts.

Stockinette Stitch (worked in the rnd)
All Rnds: Knit all sts.

Stockinette Stitch (worked flat)
Row 1 (RS): Knit all sts.
Row 2 (WS): Purl all sts.

Techniques

Provisional Cast On

With smooth waste yarn and a crochet hook, chain a few more stitches than you will be casting on. Cut the waste yarn and pull it through the last stitch to secure the chain. Insert a knitting needle into the first bump on the back of the chain, and using the yarn you will use for your sweater, pick up a stitch. Continue picking up one stitch per bump until you have the correct number of stitches on your knitting needle.

When you're ready to work the cast-on stitches, use the knitting needle to pick up the right side of each stitch. When you have all the stitches on your needle, remove the crocheted chain by untying the end and gently unraveling the whole chain.

Tubular Bind Off (worked in the rnd)

This bind off takes extra time, but it's worth it for a beautifully rounded and polished look. It has three steps:
1. Create four foundation rounds.
2. Separate your stitches onto two thinner circular needles.
3. Graft your stitches using Kitchener stitch.

1. Foundation Rows

Rnds 1 & 3: Slip marker. Knit each knit stitch and slip each purl stitch with yarn in front.
Rnds 2 & 4: Slip marker. Purl every purl stitch and slip every knit stitch with yarn in back.

2. Separating Stitches

Do not work the stitches in this step—just slip them. Hold the two thinner circular needles in your right hand, parallel to each other, tips pointing to the left. With the right side facing you, hold your working needle in your left hand, tip pointing to the right. Slip a knit stitch to the front needle, untwisted. Next, slip a purl stitch to the back needle, untwisted. Continue slipping stitches in this way until all of your stitches have been separated. You should have half the stitches (the knits) on the front needle, and half the stitches on the back needle.

3. Grafting

Keep the two sets of stitches you wish to graft on the two separate knitting needles, needles on top of each other, purl sides of the fabric together, with the tips of both of the ndls pointing to your right. Move the back needle up a little higher than the front needle so you can see a row of the stitches below the needle. If it's not already there, attach about 20 inches/51 cm of yarn to the first stitch on the back needle. Join additional lengths of yarn as needed. Thread the yarn on your tapestry needle.

1. Insert tapestry needle knitwise into the first stitch on the front needle and slip the stitch off.
2. Insert tapestry needle purlwise into second stitch on the front needle and draw the yarn through, leaving the loop on the knitting needle, switch the yarn to the back.
3. Insert the tapestry needle purlwise into the first stitch on the back loop, and slip the stitch off.
4. Insert the tapestry needle knitwise into the second stitch on the back loop, draw the yarn through, leaving the loop on the knitting needle.

Rep steps 1–4. When all the stitches have been grafted, locate the first two stitches you grafted, and connect them to the last two stitches by doing steps 3 & 4.

Contributors

Faina Goberstein
Email: faina.goberstein@gmail.com
Facebook: facebook.com/faina.goberstein
Instagram: @faina.go
Ravelry: faina-goberstein
Website: fainasknittingmode.com

Faina is a prolific knitwear designer, author, and a professional teacher. She is the coauthor of *The Art of Slip Stitch* and *The Art of Seamless Knitting*, and her designs can be found in *Vogue Knitting*, *Rowan Magazine*, *Interweave Knits*, *Knit.Purl*, *knitscene*, *Twist Collective*, and various books. Faina is best known for her elegant and well-fitted classic designs that show off textures that are created using slip-stitch patterns, cables, brioche, lace, and their combinations. Developing new slip-stitch and brioche patterns for her new designs and classes is one of Faina's interests and keeps her love for math and knitting merged.

She teaches in person at various venues nationally and abroad as well as on *Bluprint.com* and *Interweave.com*.

Juliana Lustenader
Email: lustenaderdesigns@gmail.com
Instagram: @knitbyjules
Patreon: julianalustenaderknits
Ravelry: juliana-lustenader

Jules is a knitwear designer born and raised in the SF Bay Area. Her experience working at Imagiknit helped propel her into the world of knitwear design. Her designs have been featured in multiple knitting magazines, including *Twist Collective*, *knitscene*, and *I Like Knitting*. When she is not knitting, Jules is likely performing in a local musical or play.

Audry Nicklin
Email: audry.bearears@gmail.com
Instagram: @bear_ears
Ravelry: bear-ears
Website: bear-ears.com

Audry is a Bay Area native who is best known for *Lit Knits*, a book with literature-inspired knits, as well as Celestarium, a shawl that accurately charts out all the constellations of the northern hemisphere.

Sonya Philip
Email: info@100actsofsewing.com
Instagram: @sonyaphilip
Website: 100actsofsewing.com
Ravelry: knitsonya

Sonya believes sewing and knitting make an excellent crafting pair. In 2012, she started the year long project, *100 Acts of Sewing*, and made one hundred dresses while documenting the process. Since then she has made it her mission to convince people to make and wear their own garments. Sonya lives in a drafty Victorian with her family.

Yvonne Poon
Email: info@gamerbabeknits.com
Instagram: gamerbabeknitter
Ravelry: GamerBabeKnitter

Yvonne was born and raised in San Francisco. Her mom, grandmother, and nanny all had a hand in teaching her to knit, crochet, and sew when she was little. She started designing and self-publishing her designs in 2015. Her numbers and Excel background, from working as an accountant and underwriter, have proven invaluable in her design process. Both her parents brought her to designing in their own ways. While Yvonne's mom introduced her to crafting and taught her basic craft skills, she got her love of the challenge in designing and figuring out how to make her visions work from her dad who was an electrical engineer. Many of her designs are inspired by baseball. Yvonne has been a San Francisco Giants fan since she was 12, and she finds a way to name designs after baseball players and words. She knits while watching games no matter how challenging the pattern. She loves to knit with beads and incorporates beads into her designs. Wanting warmer weather, Yvonne lives in the East Bay and works part-time at her LYS, A Yarn Less Raveled, in Danville. She still has lots of family and friends in SF.

Sloane Rosenthal
Email: rosenthalsloane@gmail.com
Instagram: @skrosenthal
Ravelry: sloane-rosenthal

Sloane Rosenthal is a California-based knitwear designer and a co-founder of Hudson + West Co. She designs modern, wearable garments and accessories, with a particular focus on cabled designs. Her work has been featured in *By Hand Serial*, *Wool Studio*, *Knit.Wear*, and *Interweave Knits*, and she is the author of three books of knitwear patterns: *Independent Fabrication Vol. 1* (2016), *Vol. 2* (2017), and *Wine Country Knits* (2018), all available from Sandreed Press. Sloane lives in the San Francisco Bay Area with her husband and two children.

Heatherly Walker
Email: heatherlywalker@gmail.com
Instagram: @yarnyenta
Ravelry: YarnYenta
Website: yarnyenta.com

Heatherly began knitting 15 years ago in a small town in Northern California called Paradise, surrounded by her 6 children who often got tangled in the skeins of yarn. The Walker Family have loved adventuring their region, from exploring lava tubes, sledding in the summer on volcanoes to high tea and gourmet ice cream in San Francisco. They have kindly indulged Heatherly's fiber addiction by finding yarn stores for her along the way. "Look, mom, there is yarn over there!" Her work has been published in *PieceWork*, *Knitting Traditions*, *The Sock Report*, and *Knitty.com*. Along with over 200 designs, she also coauthored the *Unobtainables: Fake Elements, Real Knits* book with Allison Sarnoff.

Julie Weisenberger
Email: knit@cocoknits.com
Instagram: @cocoknits
Ravelry: cocoknits
Website: cocoknits.com

Cocoknits founder, Julie, learned to knit and completed her first sweater in college while studying abroad in Salzburg, Austria. She has been knitting and designing ever since. In the 1980s she ran her own knitwear company; in the 1990s she designed sweaters for yarn companies and magazines; and in 2007 she founded *Cocoknits.com*, her own pattern and tool company. She continues to design knitwear and has created a line of tools that make the process of knitting and making easier and more beautiful. Julie teaches classes throughout the United States and in Europe. She lives in Oakland, California.

Kelly White
Email: stringandtwig@gmail.com
Instagram: @kellywhitedesigns
Ravelry: kelly-white-designs
Website: stringandtwig.com

Kelly moved to San Francisco from Los Angeles during the astonishingly rainy winter of 2005. She has enjoyed exploring Northern California and making it her home ever since. A few years ago, tired of trying to modify other peoples' patterns to suit her imagination, Kelly began publishing her own knitwear designs. She seeks to promote justice, equity, and sustainability through her work and collaborations.

Vilasinee Bunnag
Email: hello@theloome.com
Instagram: @theloome
Website: theloome.com
Ravelry: vbunnag

Vilasinee "V" Bunnag loves crafting and making. Growing up in Thailand, she was always drawn to the rich art and craft traditions of Southeast Asia. At age eleven, her art teacher in Los Angeles introduced her to knitting. It was the first time that she was exposed to yarn of any sort, since Thailand is a very hot and humid place. This exposure to yarn brought her to her current role as pom pom creator *extraordinaire*. V is an enthusiastic fiber fan, an inventor of the Loome family of tools, the founder of **Loome**, and an author of *Loome Party* (Abrams). After spending 20 years in New York City, she moved herself and Loome back to the Bay Area in 2017.

Alli Novak
Instagram: @luzography
Ravelry: Allisoleil
Website: luzography.com

Alli Novak is a Bay Area photographer, whose intimate portraits draw life and light from within her subjects. She chases bounce light and bokeh everywhere she goes. She is also a fiber aficionado, and when she isn't photographing, editing, or wrangling her two children, you can find her knitting, occasionally weaving, dubiously spinning, or helping people make color-courageous yarn choices at her LYS, The Black Squirrel. Her favorite knitting project, hands-down, is stranded colorwork. In addition to fiber-related activities, Alli loves getting her hands dirty in the garden while listening to murder mystery audiobooks, or going out on the elusive date night with her husband.

Kathleen Dames
Email: kathleen@onemorerowpress.com
Instagram: @kathleendames
Ravelry: Purly
Website: kathleendames.com

With a focus on flattering designs and knitterly details, Kathleen designs garments and accessories for her own pattern line, kathleen dames | knitwear design, as well as publications such as *Knitty*, *Jane Austen Knits*, and *Interweave Knits*. From her first large-scale knitting project, Kathleen has been making patterns her own, thanks to her personal style, the wisdom of Elizabeth Zimmermann, and the stacks of stitch dictionaries she keeps buying. On top of designing, Kathleen is cocreator of the knitting publication *Filament*, host of the podcast *The Sweater with Kathleen Dames*, and cofounder with Alice O'Reilly of **One More Row Press**.

Alice O'Reilly
Email: alice@onemorerowpress.com
Instagram: @backyardfiberworks
Ravelry: AliceOKnitty
Website: backyardfiberworks.com

Alice has always been a maker. A serious dyed in the wool, hot glue burns on her fingertips, glitter in her eyebrows maker. So when she first thought about dyeing yarn, it was in the context of making stuff to support her knitting habit. She fired up her first dye pot and, wow, was it not what she expected. True to form, she did no research. It was way too light and way too dark and way too not what was expected. But, also true to form, she kept trying. Alice threw a few more skeins in the pot. She read a few (okay a lot, she works at a library) of books about dyeing and yarn and how the two work together. Alice joined Ravelry groups and marveled at everyone else's perfect skeins. She started stalking hand-dyers on Instagram and Etsy. And then slowly she started getting more predictable results. More repeatable colorways. And it turns out she loved playing with color as much as she loved playing with yarn. And that's how **Backyard Fiberworks** began. Soon after they met, Alice and Kathleen started talking about collaborating, and before they knew it, they were making a knitting book about New York City as **One More Row Press**.

Thanks!

Scott Territo & Kanyon Sayers-Roods
for crafting our land acknowledgment

Kelly White for connecting us and working with Kanyon and Scott and for teaching us more about Ruth Asawa

Laura Cameron for technical editing

Laurel Johnson for our illustrations

Bhavana Srinivas & Gowtham Ramachandran for modeling

Ryan James & Gowtham Ramachandran for assisting on the photo shoots

Our family & friends
for their love and support

Pattern Index

Continuous, p. 9
Sincere Sheep Favor

Ferry Building, p. 15
Hudson + West Co. WELD

Fog City, p. 21
Sincere Sheep Covet DK

Grant Avenue Stroll, p. 25
The Dye Project Montara DK

Half-Moon, p. 31
Love Fest Fibers Tough Love Tiny

Lombard Street, p. 35
Bay Street Yarns Ava

Mission Dolores, p. 39
Speckled Finch Studios Bouncy DK

Painted Lady, p. 43
Twirl Yarn Ditto

Yerba Buena, p. 47
A Verb for Keeping Warm Gather

18th & Castro, p. 51
Little Skein in the Big Wool House Sock

Happy knitting!

www.ingramcontent.com/pod-product-compliance
Lightning Source LLC
Chambersburg PA
CBHW041157290426
44108CB00003B/100